Pre-Fall Marriage

God's Original Will

A Workbook of Main Points and Probing Questions

Rick and Georgeann Mills

PreFallMarriage.com
or
https://www.facebook.com/PreFallMarriage

Version 1.00

Cover artwork: Marriages Through the Fire

ISBN 978-0-9862236-1-7

RF Publishing
Ames, IA 50014

ALSO BY RICK AND GEORGEANN MILLS

Pre-Fall Marriage God's Original Will: A Journey by Email
to a Mutually Satisfying Marriage

https://Pre-FallMarriage.com

ALSO BY RICK MILLS

The Yoke of Jesus: If His Yoke Is Easy,
Why Can Life Be So Difficult

https://TheYokeOfJesus.com

PREFACE

This workbook of main points and probing questions is a companion to the novel, Pre-Fall Marriage God's Original Will – A Journey by Email to a Mutually Satisfying Marriage. The novel is about Jack and Caroline's journey with Rick and Georgeann to a Pre-Fall mutually satisfying marriage.

The story has been removed and what remains are the main points from each email, along with probing Me Questions to be answered individually and We Questions to be answered as a couple. Some of the main points will appear in multiple emails because they are discussed and reinforced to varying levels of detail throughout the story. There is also a Your Thoughts section after each set of questions.

You may choose to write your answers to the questions and your thoughts in this workbook, or you may want to consider using a separate journal for privacy and more flexibility in the length of your responses.

While the purpose of this workbook and the novel is primarily to help married and engaged couples with their personal and marriage-related struggles, individuals in various types and stages of relationships will also find this material beneficial.

People who are divorced can use this material to not only understand relationships from their past, but also to build a mutually satisfying marriage in the future. People who are single can use this material to understand the mental and emotional dynamics of their current and past relationships, as well as the relationships of others such as parents, family, and friends. And finally, anyone who is committed to helping couples heal and grow through marriage will find this workbook to be a useful resource.

The main points and probing questions in this workbook may be unpleasant to read and consider. Our purpose is not to open mental and emotional wounds unnecessarily, but rather, to shed light on areas that cause pain and difficulty in marriage relationships. The pain and difficulty that many couples go through is not surprising based on the marriages they have seen, and the role models who taught them what to think and how to act in a marriage.

Even though you can benefit from using this workbook on your own, we encourage you to do so with your spouse, a friend, or a study group, so together, you can pray and work through the thoughts and feelings that arise. It is often in the eyes of someone you trust that the truth of your past experiences is reflected more accurately than what you can perceive on your own. That said, anything from someone else that you receive into your thinking must be in alignment with Scripture, and also be consistent with your discernment from the Holy Spirit.

This workbook provides educational insight and is not offered as a therapeutic process or any form of therapy. If reading the main points and/or answering the questions triggers strong and potentially overwhelming emotions from your current or past circumstances, please take a break from reading, put yourself first, and establish a therapeutic relationship with a qualified mental health professional.

If you ever feel like you may physically harm yourself or someone else, call a trusted family member, friend, Christian brother or sister, pastor, counselor, or psychiatrist. In an emergency, either call your local emergency service (usually 9-1-1 in the United States), or a law enforcement agency. You may also go to the nearest emergency room on your own, or have someone take you. You are precious in God's eyes and worthy of the care you need.

As part of our desire to continue with you on your journey to a Pre-Fall mutually satisfying marriage, we have created a companion website, **https://Pre-FallMarriage.com,** and a page on Facebook, **https://www.facebook.com/PreFallMarriage**. At these two sites we will periodically offer additional thoughts on marriage based on our personal growth, and comments from you and others. If you have insights or helpful suggestions that you would like to share, we would love to hear from you.

The main points and probing questions in this workbook are not in reference to any specific person or event. All characters in the novel are fictional except for Rick and Georgeann. Any other names, characters, businesses, places, events, locales, and incidents are either the products of Rick or Georgeann's imagination, or used in a fictitious manner. Specific references to people or events are used by permission.

Blessings by the power of the Holy Spirit on your journey to build a mutually satisfying marriage.

Rick and Georgeann

DEDICATION

———————

This workbook is dedicated to you as you live out your journey of healing and growth through a mutually satisfying marriage. Your courage and the choices you make will change your destiny and the destiny of your family and others for generations. You matter and your healing and growth matters to God as He conforms you into your unique image of Jesus. The mutually satisfying marriage that you build with your spouse matters to a watching world who needs hope, direction, and peace.

May God bless you as you grow in wisdom, gentleness, and perseverance on your journey.

OVERVIEW

Background

This workbook of main points and probing questions is a companion to the novel, Pre-Fall Marriage God's Original Will - A Journey by Email to a Mutually Satisfying Marriage.

In the novel, Jack and Caroline are missionaries serving in a very remote location with intermittent connectivity to the internet. They love each other, but argue constantly. They will not be coming back to the States until they complete their current tour, and have asked Rick and Georgeann for help. Since the four of them cannot meet face to face, and the use of video conferencing is impossible, Rick and Georgeann have agreed to attempt the very unusual task of helping them by email. The result is an exchange of emails about God's purpose for healing and growth through their marriage, and how Jack's and Caroline's wounds and defenses contribute to their arguments. Jack and Caroline learn strategies and tools for building a mutually satisfying marriage. They also receive a Conflict Checklist for identifying factors that are contributing to their arguments.

Pre-Fall Marriage

God made his original will for Adam and Eve's relationship clear when He said,

> …"Let us make mankind in our image, in our likeness, so that they may rule over the fish in the sea and the birds in the sky, over the livestock and all the wild animals, and over all the creatures that move along the ground." [27] So God created mankind in his own image, in the image of God he created them; male and female he created them. (Genesis 1:26-27)

The "mankind" to which God referred was Adam and Eve, and together they were given rule "over the fish in the sea and the birds in the sky, over the livestock and all the wild animals, and over all the creatures that move along the ground." Adam's rule over Eve came only after the Fall when Satan injected his will into the Garden, causing God to speak to them in Genesis 3:16. '"To the woman he said, "I will make your pains in childbearing very severe; with painful labor you will give birth to children. Your desire will be for your husband, and he will rule over you."'

The beauty, love, and power that was built into Adam and Eve as the image of the "us" who were present at creation became distorted into a struggle for power in the presence of pain.

What happened to God's original will for marriage?

In the Sermon on the Mount, Jesus taught what has become known as the Lord's Prayer.

"This, then, is how you should pray:

"'Our Father in heaven, hallowed be your name,
[10] your kingdom come, your will be done,
    on earth as it is in heaven.
[11] Give us today our daily bread.
[12] And forgive us our debts,
    as we also have forgiven our debtors.
[13] And lead us not into temptation,
    but deliver us from the evil one.' (Matthew 6:9-13)

When Jesus said in verse 10, "your kingdom come, your will be done on earth as it is in heaven," we think He meant this literally. But, this raises the question, "What is God's heavenly will for an earthly marriage?"

We believe that God's heavenly will for an earthly marriage is to build it on a Pre-Fall foundation where spouses are once again coequal in their created image of God. This stands in direct contrast to those who advocate building a marriage on the fallen rubble of first century Roman culture where a wife was the property of her husband.

A problem arises, however, in that there isn't a lot recorded in Scripture about the rules and behaviors that Adam and Eve were to live by in their Pre-Fall marriage. And, why would there be? They knew all they needed to know, and what they knew was all good. They were without sin because of their lack of knowledge about good and evil. They had no selfish desires, unmet needs, fears, wounds, defenses, or assumptions. Today, such is not the case for Christians and their marriages.

Even though people become a new creation when they accept Jesus as their Savior, God retains their old brain. This brain has a mind that includes finely tuned time-tested rules, behaviors, and instincts for survival. These instincts are near-instantaneous in their reaction time, and are driven by desires, needs, fears, past and present wounds, defenses, and assumptions. A transformation of this mind and these instincts is needed.

God wants your desires purified, needs met, fears confronted, wounds healed, defenses removed, and assumptions challenged. He wants your instincts reexamined, your rules rewritten, and your behaviors redirected so you can walk in wisdom, love, self-discipline, and power. (2 Timothy 1:7). In fact, God's will is the same for everyone in that He wants to conform everyone into their own unique image of Jesus. (Romans 8:29)

One of the tools God uses to bring about this conformation is a marriage relationship. To that end, we believe a primary purpose of marriage is healing and growth, and that one spouse's desires and needs can be signals for areas in which God wants the other to grow. It is by this growth that those desires and needs can be met. This begins with both spouses offering themselves to God as a living sacrifice.

> Therefore, I urge you, brothers and sisters, in view of God's mercy, to offer your bodies as a living sacrifice, holy and pleasing to God—this is your true and proper worship. [2] Do not conform to the pattern of this world, but be transformed by the renewing of your mind. Then you will be able to test and approve what God's will is—his good, pleasing and perfect will. (Romans 12:1-2)

Many people *go to* God's altar to pray for what is on their mind, and when finished, leave and work hard at bringing about what they desire. In essence, they ask God to bless their efforts the way rain blesses a farmer. This is not what Romans 12:1-2 is urging.

God wants you to *climb up onto* His altar and offer yourself as a *living* sacrifice. This is the kind of worship that pleases Him. It allows Him to address the ways you have been conformed to this world, and it allows Him to transform you by renewing your mind. As your mind is renewed, you will become more and more confident in knowing what He wants you to do.

God does not want you *working for Him*, rather, He wants to *work through you*. This does not take away your freedom and responsibility, rather, it frees you to respond to God as your loving Father and not as a harsh taskmaster. When God works through you as you rest in Him, you arise with love, strength, and power.

So where is the specific guidance found in the Bible for spouses who want to build a Pre-Fall marriage? It is the same guidance that Scripture offers on how we as Christians should interact with one another and those around us.

We believe God wants husbands to treat their wives at least as well and even better than they treat anyone else, and He wants wives to do the same with their husbands. Therefore, Scriptures such as Luke 6:27 that say you should love your enemies could be appended with, "… and love your spouse with the same love and even more than what I am commanding you to have for your enemies." Scriptures such as Ephesians 4:15 that say you should speak the truth in love could be appended with, "… and speak the truth to your spouse with the same love and even more than you should have for a fellow believer." This means that specific guidance for a Pre-Fall marriage is found throughout Scripture.

Your journey using this workbook

If you and your spouse use this workbook, success will not be achieved merely by reading through the main points and questions. It is by reading, thinking, praying, working through the questions, discussing, and putting your insights into practice that the two of you will experience the often painful process of healing and growth, along with the joyful process of building and experiencing your own mutually satisfying marriage.

There are at least six requirements for success: desire, opportunity, time, energy, courage, and insight.

Both you and your spouse must grow in your *desire* for a mutually satisfying marriage and be willing to offer each other the *opportunity* for connection. If one or both of you are closed off mentally and/or emotionally to the other, your journey is in peril. Both of you must also set aside the necessary *time* for this journey, and allow the Holy Spirit to work in and through you as He provides the *energy*.

In addition, both of you need to grow in your *courage* to examine your past relationships and the impact that those relationships have had on you and your current relationships. Each of you must also grow in your *courage* to examine your mental and emotional struggles as individuals and as a couple.

And finally, you will need *insight* into your automatic survival instincts that protect your mental and emotional wounds. We can provide some insight with this workbook, and you must either bring or be willing to grow in the other requirements.

Try not to lose sight of the fact that even though God's path for your journey to a mutually satisfying marriage will be painful, the outcome of healing and growth and of being conformed to your unique image of Jesus is worth it.

In Him,

Rick and Georgeann

Subject: Hello
Main Points

Look at each other when you talk.

Treat your spouse in a way that shows she or he really matters to you.

Show affection and touch each other.

A disagreement does not have to escalate into an argument.

Family of origin dynamics can vary considerably between spouses.

Identifying one's life purpose can occur at an early age.

Excellence in one area of your life does not compensate for being underdeveloped in others, such as the ability to understand feelings and communicate with your spouse.

Agreeing to do something does not mean you understand the impending challenge or pain.

Apologize when you are wrong.

Speak the truth in love. Secrets between spouses are rarely helpful.

People who are relationally challenged can still love God and their family, and serve others effectively while they continue to grow.

Sometimes God's path for you is painful.

Me Questions

1) In what ways do you treat your spouse that shows she or he matters to you?

   _____

   _____

   _____

2) How do you show affection? How do you like to be shown affection?

   _____

   _____

   _____

3) Do you have a sense of your life purpose? If so, what is it at this time? What are your strengths? (No need for false humility)

_____

_____

4) What are your weaknesses? (No need for self-condemnation)

_____

_____

5) Are you able to apologize when you are wrong? If not, why?

_____

_____

6) What have you agreed to do in your life that turned out to be more challenging and painful than you thought it would be? Why was it so?

_____

_____

7) What does speaking the truth in love mean to you?

_____

_____

We Questions

8) What contributes to the escalation of your disagreements into arguments?

_____

_____

9) How do the dynamics of your families of origin differ? How do those differences impact your relationship?

_____

_____

Your Thoughts

_____

_____

_____

_____

_____

_____

_____

_____

_____

_____

_____

_____

_____

_____

_____

_____

Subject: Re: Hello; Couples, Spinning Plates, and Happiness
Main Points

Pay attention and learn from your mistakes and the mistakes of others.

Building a mutually satisfying marriage is a journey.

You can learn from others, but do not try to imitate someone else's marriage relationship. The two of you must build your own unique mutually satisfying marriage.

Couples do the work

Words often carry deep and subtle meanings.

Marriage coaches/counselors/friends can offer a different perspective and awareness, surface God's wisdom, provide honest stories of success and failure, and facilitate the moving of the Holy Spirit.

A healthy marriage requires courage, humility, hard work, submission to God's insight and wisdom, and a yielding to the power of the Holy Spirit.

In order to have a healthy marriage, you must face longstanding desires, needs, fears, wounds, defenses, and assumptions.

A couple or not a couple

Couples counseling can help two people who are a couple, and not those who are in an abusive relationship where one or both spouses try to manipulate the other.

An abusive relationship is one in which there is a power struggle for one or both spouses to manipulate and deform the other into what he or she wants without regard for the other's desires and needs. In this circumstance, an abuser must first receive effective individual counseling before entering into couples counseling.

You must continually work hard to understand each other's desires, needs, fears, wounds, defenses, and assumptions. Your relationship must be and feel safe.

The majority of arguments stem directly from unmet desires, unacknowledged needs, unresolved fears, past wounds, clashing defenses, and unyielding assumptions. And, all of these are amplified by the daily pressures of life.

God's will for each of us and a purpose for marriage

God wants your desires purified, needs met, fears confronted, wounds healed, defenses removed, and assumptions examined.

God wants you to walk in wisdom, love, self-discipline, and power. (2 Timothy 1:7)

God's will is the same for everyone as recorded in Romans 8:29, "For those God foreknew he also predestined to be conformed to the image of his Son, that he might be the firstborn among many brothers and sisters." This means that you are continuously being conformed by God into your own unique image of Jesus.

A primary purpose of your marriage is healing and growth for you and your spouse.

A spouse's desire is often a need for the relationship

Gently and purposefully embrace your unhappiness and discontent. Look for insight that will be helpful in your healing and growth.

Your spouse's desires and needs can be signals for areas in which God wants you to grow.

Ask God to give you insight into your desires and needs.

Your spouse's need is often what is needed for your relationship.

Refusing to tell your spouse about a felt desire or need does harm to your relationship. Refusing to listen to your spouse when she or he is telling you about a felt desire or need does harm as well.

The purpose of your marriage is not to satisfy all of your hidden desires, especially the holdovers from childhood. Hidden desires include, "Ah, finally someone to love me like my mother and father would not" or "All of my childhood insecurities will go away because I have found the *perfect spouse*."

Everyone enters into marriage with assumptions about their spouse.

When hidden desires are not fulfilled, a spouse can feel ripped off.

When hidden desires are finally revealed, the other spouse can feel deceived.

If your marriage is unsatisfying, your choice is to either look around for a *better deal* with someone else, or muster the courage through the power of the Holy Spirit to examine your desires, needs, fears, wounds, defenses, and assumptions, as well as those of your spouse.

Courageously reexamine everything

Courageously reexamine yourself and your marriage relationship in light of God's truth.

All of your desires are not selfish, all of your needs are not permanent, all of your fears are not unjustified, all of your wounds are not imagined, all of your defenses are not unnecessary, and all of your assumptions are not unreasonable. The problem is that these can get in the way of what you want more, which is a satisfying marriage.

Your healing and growth will be painful, messy, frustrating, and worth it.

It took a lifetime for you to get where you are, and it will require time, commitment, courage, and hard work to build a mutually satisfying marriage.

Some of your previous relationship experiences can be helpful in building a mutually satisfying marriage, while others, not so much. It is critical for you to identify and change unfruitful patterns.

Insight, tools, and being a living sacrifice

The two of you will either deal with your pain, or pass it on to your children, family, and friends.

The two of you need insight and tools to work through your painful past along with its current impact on your marriage.

Trying to build a healthy marriage without insight and tools is like trying to build a house without plans, while using your forehead as a hammer. Eventually the pain becomes too great to continue.

Building a healthy marriage begins with both of you offering yourself to God as a living sacrifice.

> Therefore, I urge you, brothers and sisters, in view of God's mercy, to offer your bodies as a living sacrifice, holy and pleasing to God—this is your true and proper worship. 2 Do not conform to the pattern of this world, but be transformed by the renewing of your mind. Then you will be able to test and approve what God's will is—his good, pleasing and perfect will. (Romans 12:1-2)

Climb up onto God's altar and offer yourself as a *living* sacrifice. This is the kind of worship that pleases Him.

As your mind is renewed, you will become more and more confident in what he wants you to do.

God does not want you *working for Him*, rather, He wants to *work through you*. This does not take away your freedom and responsibility, rather, it frees you to respond to God as your loving Father and not as a harsh taskmaster.

When you rest in God, you arise with love, strength, and power.

Spinning plates

Life can be like spinning plates on sticks that you have to run from one to another to keep them spinning so they won't fall.

It is a mistake to view your spouse, children, or God, as just more plates that need spinning.

Keeping up with spinning plates can make you tired, frustrated, and impatient.

Vince Lombardi once said, "Fatigue makes cowards of us all." It might not make you a "coward," but it can make you feel angry, inadequate, and at times, mean.

From time to time everyone says "stupid" things.

Making someone happy

You cannot make your spouse happy, though your actions can definitely make him or her unhappy with you.

Your happiness is between you and God.

It is your responsibility to act in a godly loving way towards your spouse, and it is your spouse's responsibility and choice to respond appropriately.

Expressing emotions

It is not true that whoever gets emotional first loses.

Emotional does not necessarily mean irrational and wrong. It can mean provoked and right.

Men often hide behind a seemingly righteous and unemotional shield of logic, while women are often looking for validation of their concerns and an emotional connection.

Men often think they are not emotional if they do not express their emotions, yet women know those emotions exist and are boiling under the surface.

Men who value constraining their emotions, often devalue women who do not, and use that as a convenient excuse to dismiss their concerns.

Still Face Experiment with a mother and her infant – Face-to-face connection and cooing brings about a pleasant contentment, while showing no expression by the mother provokes the baby to frustration and anger.

When one spouse is perceived as cold and emotionally disconnected, the other can get anxious, irritated, and angry to the point of demanding a connection by becoming more and more emotional.

Long-term hope

Restoring a single marriage to what God intended changes the destiny of that family and others for generations.

Pray and put your insights into practice.

Every day you are offered a thousand more urgent things to do than work on your marriage.

Each day that nothing changes, nothing changes.

The two of you need to make the difficult choice to face you pain together.

It's what you do with insight in the power of the Holy Spirit that will change your life and the lives of those you love.

Share with others the insights that God gives you about your marriage.

Me Questions

1) Do you have the courage and humility to do the hard work of building a mutually satisfying marriage based on God's insight and wisdom in the power of the Holy Spirit? If not, what is next for your marriage?

2) What mistakes have you made in previous relationships?

3) What mistakes have you seen others make in relationships?

4) What does the marriage you want to build look like? Is it mutually satisfying for your spouse?

5) After asking God for insight, what are your long standing desires, needs, fears, wounds, defenses, and assumptions?

6) Do you believe God wants your desires purified, needs met, fears confronted, wounds healed, defenses removed, and assumptions examined? If not, why?

7) Are you mentally, emotionally, spiritually, and/or physically abusive to your spouse? If so, in what ways and why?

_____

_____

8) Would your spouse say you are mentally, emotionally, spiritually and/or physically abusive? If so, in what ways and why?

_____

_____

9) Are you being mentally, emotionally, spiritually, and/or physically abused? If so, in what ways and why?

_____

_____

10) After talking with your spouse and asking God for insight, what are your spouse's long standing desires, needs, fears, wounds, defenses, and assumptions?

_____

_____

11) What do you think about the statement, "God wants you to walk in wisdom, love, self-discipline, and power"? (2 Timothy 1:7). How can you walk this way in your marriage?

_____

_____

12) What do you believe about the statement, "God's will is the same for everyone in that He wants to conform everyone into their own unique image of His Son"? (Romans 8:29)

_____

_____

13) What do you believe about the statement, "A primary purpose of your marriage is healing and growth for you and your spouse"?

_____

_____

14) What do you believe about the statement, "Your desires and needs can be signals for areas in which God wants *your spouse* to grow so he or she can respond to them"?

_____

_____

15) What do you think about the statement, "Your spouse's desires and needs can be signals for areas in which God wants *you* to grow so you can respond to them"?

_____

_____

16) How can you gently and purposefully embrace your unhappiness and discontent?

_____

_____

17) Is the purpose of your marriage to satisfy all of your desires, especially the holdovers from your childhood? If not, what do you do with those desires?

_____

_____

18) What do you believe about the statement, "Your healing and growth will be painful, messy, frustrating, and worth it"?

_____

_____

19) What previous relationship experiences have you had that are helpful to your marriage? In what ways are they helpful?

_____

_____

20) What previous relationship experiences have you had that are not helpful to your marriage? In what ways are they not helpful?

_____

_____

21) What do you believe about the statement, "The two of you will either deal with your pain, or pass it on to your children, family, and friends"?

_____

_____

22) What tools and plans are you using to build your marriage?

_____

_____

23) Are you comfortable with the idea of offering yourself to God as a living sacrifice? If not, why? What would offering yourself to God look like in your day-to-day experience?

_____

_____

24) What does it mean for God to want to *work through you,* rather than for you to *work for Him?*

_____

_____

25) What does "rest in God" mean to you?

_____

_____

26) Do you treat people like they are spinning plates on sticks that you have to keep spinning? If so, who are they and in what ways do you have to keep them spinning?

_____

_____

27) Does trying to keep your plates spinning leave you feeling tired, frustrated, impatient, angry, or mean? If so, what can you do differently?

_____

_____

28) What do you believe about the statement, "You cannot make your spouse happy, though your actions can definitely make him or her unhappy with you"?

_____

_____

29) What do you think about the statement, "Your happiness is between you and God"?

_____

_____

30) What are your thoughts about the statement, "It is your responsibility to act in a godly loving way towards your spouse, and it is your spouse's choice to respond appropriately"?

_____

_____

31) What do you think about the statement, "Whoever gets emotional first loses"?

_____

_____

32) What do you believe about the statement, "A person who gets emotional is irrational and wrong"?

_____

_____

33) Is it possible that people who are emotional may be provoked and right? Have you experienced this in your marriage? If so, how?

_____

_____

34) What do you think about the statement, "Men often hide behind a seemingly righteous and unemotional shield of logic, while women are often looking for validation of their concerns and an emotional connection"? Is this true in your marriage? If so, why? Do you know couples where this is reversed and the woman has a shield of logic? If so, how do they handle this difference?

_____

_____

_____

_____

_____

35) What are your thoughts about the statement, "Your spouse is not emotional if he or she does not express his or her emotions"?

_____

_____

36) Do you devalue and dismiss the concerns of your spouse if he or she does not constrain his or her emotions? If so, why? Who taught you to do this?

_____

_____

37) During a disagreement, do you act cold and emotionless toward your spouse? If so, why? Is it for protection or to make your spouse get anxious, irritated, and angry?

_____

_____

38) What do you believe about the statement, "Restoring a single marriage to what God intended changes the destiny of that family and others for generations s"? What do you think God intends for your marriage?

_____

_____

39) Are you able to pray with your spouse, talk about the insights in this book, and work together to put them into practice? If not, what is your plan for improving your marriage?

_____

_____

_____

_____

_____

40) List 10 things that are more urgent than working on your marriage. How will they be impacted if you cannot build a mutually satisfying marriage?

_____

_____

41) What do you believe about the statement, "Each day that nothing changes, nothing changes"?

_____

_____

42) What do you think about the statement, "It is what you do with insight in the power of the Holy Spirit that will change your life and the lives of those you love"? Have you ever seen insight not bring about change? If so, when and what happened?

_____

_____

43) Are you willing to face your mental and emotional pain with the help of your spouse? How can you do this? Do you need help from a professional? If so, who could help you?

_____

_____

44) Are you willing to help your spouse face his or her mental and emotional pain? How can you do this? If not, what is your plan for the future?

_____

_____

_____

_____

We Questions

45) Are you trying to manipulate each other? If so, how effective has it been and how long will the two of you keep trying to doing so?

_____

_____

_____

46) Are the two of you in a power struggle? If so, how is it leading to a *mutually* satisfying marriage?

_____

_____

47) Does either of you feel like you are in an abusive relationship in which there is a power struggle for one or both of you to manipulate and deform the other into what you want without regard for the other's desires and needs? If you feel that way, how might life be better if one or both of you tried a different strategy of working on yourself and not on your spouse? This begins by offering yourself to God as a living sacrifice.

_____

_____

48) Are you willing to share with other couples the insights that God gives the two of you about your marriage? What insights would you currently offer?

_____

_____

Your Thoughts

_____

_____

_____

_____

_____

_____

_____

_____

_____

Subject: Arguing, Needs, Love, and Respect
Main Points

Being open about feelings in some families can be dangerous.

Admit it when you are wrong.

Calmly speaking unemotional statements is not necessarily less damaging than yelling them.

Some people feel completely selfish when they focus on themselves.

Me Questions

1) Was being open about your feelings in your family of origin dangerous? If so, which feelings and in what way was it dangerous?

   _____

   _____

2) Do you admit it when you are wrong? If not, why?

   _____

   _____

3) Do you believe it is wrong to focus on yourself? If so, why?

   _____

   _____

We Question

4) When you are arguing with each other, how damaging are your words?

   _____

   _____

Your Thoughts

_____

_____

_____

_____

_____

_____

_____

_____

_____

_____

Subject: Your Observing Ego and Shame
Main Points

Observing ego

Changing how you interact with others begins with the ability to accurately observe yourself while you are in the process of interacting. Some refer to this as an observing ego.

A healthy observing ego is the capacity to accurately observe yourself while you are interacting with others, and to later reflect upon those interactions.

Your observing ego is a continuous awareness that observes your thoughts, emotions, and attitudes, as well as your strategies and their implementation for getting what you want.

Some refer to the observing ego as one's conscience or "the parent within."

Your observing ego sounds like a running narrative of thought that is commenting on what you feel, think, say, and do.

Those who refer to the observing ego as "the parent within" often make it sound like it is a separate person (a child's parent) that is imported into his or her mind that must either be accepted or rejected.

Others refer to the observing ego as "tapes," which are today's equivalent of an MP3. These recordings, that play in their mind, sound like what their parents said to them when they were growing up, be it praise or judgment.

Regardless of what you call your observing ego, you experience its presence.

You own your observing ego and can change its rules based on God's truth and wisdom from others.

The rules for your observing ego are derived from childhood and adulthood relationships in which parents, caregivers, friends, a spouse or ex-spouse, and others such as teachers and coaches tell you what is right or wrong for you to think, and what is appropriate or not for you to do.

Your observing ego uses its rules to determine whether you are good or bad, and if your behavior is appropriate or not.

The health of your observing ego and its rationale is influenced heavily by the mental, emotional, and spiritual health of those significant individuals from whom you acquired your rules.

Unreliable rules of your observing ego that are unchallenged remain as truth.

Children who do not experience forgiveness by a parent or caregiver have no reason to include a rule in their observing ego that God or anyone else will be forgiving.

Implanting life-giving rules or injecting those that are toxic happens easily with children because they are naïve and believe what they are told.

The best rule provider for your observing ego is Scripture and what God says about you. What matters is what He says is right or wrong, and appropriate or not.

Your observing ego keeps you aware of your emotions, and watches for attitudes that can arise from the activation of your wounds.

Once you know your spouse's wounds, you can either be gentle and merciful, or harsh and condemning. You can either lovingly speak words of healing into your spouse's wounds, or savagely thrust your verbal sword into them.

Be aware of how your spouse is responding based on facial expressions and body language.

When arguing with your spouse, ask yourself if your spouse is understanding what you are saying.

Ask yourself if you are understanding what your spouse is saying.

Of even more importance, ask yourself if *you* are understanding what *you* are saying.

Your observing ego allows you to be engaged in an interaction both as a participant and as an observer.

The angrier you get during an argument, the more shut down your observing ego becomes.

When you become instantly furious with your spouse or someone else, it often has to do with re-opening a childhood wound.

A response is always better than a reaction.

A condemning observing ego

A healthy observing ego lets you know when you have done something right or wrong.

An unhealthy observing ego is an unreliable observer whose conclusions are flawed.

If the rules of your observing ego are condemning, you will condemn yourself for anything you do for any reason, or no reason at all. You will always believe that what you do isn't good enough, or done soon enough, or not whatever enough.

According to a condemning observing ego, you are always bad and deserving of punishment and rejection.

Relentless harsh self-judgments can result in a constant sense of guilt, badness, and shame.

Narcissists

Narcissists have an observing ego that has no room for guilt or badness and the resulting shame.

A narcissist is completely comfortable spewing blame and shame on someone else for anything and everything that does not turn out exactly as desired.

If you accept a narcissist's shame, you become his or her shame bearer.

If you are a shame bearer for a narcissist, you end up feeling bad about yourself because you are wearing the narcissist's shame, which has nothing to do with your own.

Narcissists do not keep people around who do not accept this shame transfer, and who insist on holding them accountable for their words and actions. If you refuse to bear their shame, you will be discarded like a used tissue.

Trying to confess inappropriate shame

If you try to confess inappropriate shame to God, meaning that which was spewed onto you from someone else, it is very difficult for you to *experience* God's forgiveness. The reason is that you can only claim the *real blood* of Jesus for your own *real sin*, not the *imagined sin* that has been shamed onto you from someone else, or even inappropriately from yourself.

For example, you cannot confess and receive forgiveness from God for being condemning and judgmental if the basis for your belief is that you were told you were that way by a condemning and judgmental person. In reality, it is much more likely that your accuser is projecting his or her own condemning and judgmental character onto you.

What can make you vulnerable to receiving this type of inappropriate shame is that, at times, you probably can be condemning and judgmental. If you combine this truth with a desire to be humble and authentic with God, and then add the convincing sincerity of your accuser, you can end up experiencing a confusing and non-resolving sense of self-condemnation and self-judgment for thinking you are condemning and judgmental. Those feelings of inappropriate shame would not be from God.

If you are experiencing someone else's shame, what you need is not forgiveness, rather, you need a renewing of your mind such that you do not receive their shame in the first place.

Renewing your mind

> Therefore, I urge you, brothers and sisters, in view of God's mercy, to offer your bodies as a living sacrifice, holy and pleasing to God—this is your true and proper worship. [2] Do not conform to the pattern of this world, but be transformed by the renewing of your mind. Then you

will be able to test and approve what God's will is—his good, pleasing and perfect will. (Romans 12:1-2)

You need to offer yourself to God as a living sacrifice for the renewing of your mind, not offer yourself to someone else for its continued distortion by their shame.

It is only by offering yourself to God that you will be able to test and approve what His will is by His rules, and not succumb to the will of others by their rules.

The renewal of your mind is to *no longer accept* the inappropriate shame of others, or the toxic rules that were injected into you by unreliable rule-providers.

Seeking forgiveness for inappropriate shame does not result in the experience of change and true freedom.

Change and true freedom for a shame bearer only occurs with a renewing of the mind that is no longer vulnerable to receiving and believing the inappropriate shame of others.

When someone tries to project inappropriate shame onto you, you can either think the timid and submissive thought of "Well, this person might be right. I should apologize," or the bold and authoritative thought of, "No, this person is wrong! I refuse to receive anyone's shame!"

Healthy narcissism

Healthy narcissism allows you to enjoy and experience satisfaction in your accomplishments, while also taking responsibility for the outcome when you do not do something well.

God has no problem with you enjoying your accomplishments and finding satisfaction, as long as your accomplishments and that satisfaction do not displace Him.

Humility is not the absence of healthy narcissism, it is praising God and giving Him the glory in the midst of it.

The health of an observing ego is on a continuum

The health of your observing ego is on a continuum and can vary depending on the area of your life. These areas include work, recreation, ministry, marriage, parenting, etc. Growth in one area usually brings about progress in the others.

God wants your observing ego to grow in all areas of your life. To this end, you are constantly adding, refining, or removing rules through experience, insight, and the power of the Holy Spirit.

Once your observing ego has rules that are healthy enough and reliable enough to be useful, you can use its observations to develop skills for interacting with others.

When you are in a disagreement or even an argument with your spouse, participate and observe without becoming immersed and losing your perspective.

Look for ways that you or your spouse may have contributed to an argument without either of you being wrong and deserving of blame and shame.

When you find yourself in an argument with your spouse, remain creative and thoughtful, looking for ways to deescalate the argument back to the original conflict and misalignment of perspectives. This can only occur by talking and listening with the goal of understanding.

Remember what helps each of you understand the other, and what does not.

Try to be authentically engaged with each other without fear of rejection and abandonment.

As you and your spouse develop healthier observing egos, your arguments will decrease in frequency and intensity. You will have the ability to identify your previous wounds and current issues, along with the courage to accept them as your own.

Hormones

Hormones are a very real part of being a woman…and of being a man.

Hormones come and go, and there's no sense fighting them or condemning yourself for how they make you feel.

Do not let others condemn you for the influence your hormones have on you.

Be honest with your family about the impact of your hormones.

Pregnancy can take a toll on your body that can result in negative self-talk.

Appreciate the beauty of your youth that you passed on to your children.

Even though yours and your spouse's physical body changes over the years, your body is always God's gift to your spouse, and your spouse's body is God's gift to you.

As you get older, keep learning how to physically express your intimacy and love for each other.

Me Questions

1) What is the definition of an observing ego?

_____

_____

_____

_____

_____

2) What are the rules of your observing ego?

_____

_____

_____

3) Where did, and do, you get the rules for your observing ego?

_____

_____

4) What determines the health of your observing ego?

_____

_____

5) How did childhood and adulthood experiences impact the rules of your observing ego?

_____

_____

6) Left unchallenged, unreliable rules of your observing ego remain as _____.

7) Children are naïve and have the nasty habit of _____ _____ _____ ____ _____.

8) The best rule provider is _____ and what God _____ about you.

9) How do you use your observing ego when you interact with others?

_____

_____

10) When arguing with your spouse, how likely are you to be aware of how he or she is responding or reacting by noticing facial expressions and body language? Do you care how your spouse is responding or reacting? If not, why?

_____

_____

11) When arguing with your spouse, does your observing ego care if he or she understands what you are saying, as opposed to you just wanting him or her to do what you want? If not, why

_____

_____

12) When arguing with your spouse, how often do you ask yourself if you understand what *your spouse* is saying?

_____

_____

13) When arguing with your spouse, how often do you ask yourself if you understand what *you* are saying?

_____

_____

14) How difficult is it for you to interact with someone both as a participant in the interaction and as an observer?

_____

_____

_____

15) Is it true that someone's observing ego shuts down when he or she is angry? If so, why?

_____

_____

_____

_____

16) If you believe that you can either lovingly speak words of healing into your spouse's wounds, or savagely thrust your verbal sword into them, why would you want to thrust a verbal sword into the wound of your spouse? How is this related to the power struggle?

_____

_____

17) Does it make sense that when you become instantly furious with your spouse, it often has to do with re-opening a childhood wound? If not, why?

_____

_____

_____

18) What is the difference between a response and a reaction?

_____

_____

19) When you realize you have done something wrong to your spouse, are you able to ask for forgiveness and make amends? If not, why?

_____

_____

_____

_____

20) Are the rules of your observing ego always condemning? Do you condemn yourself for anything you do for any reason, or no reason at all? If so, who taught you those rules and how did you learn them?

_____

_____

_____

_____

21) According to a *condemning* observing ego, you are always bad and deserving of punishment and rejection no matter what you do. If you had a friend who suffers from this, what would you tell him or her?

_____

_____

_____

22) Can you appropriate for yourself the same grace and mercy you would tell your friend in the question above? If not, why?

_____

_____

23) Relentless harsh self-judgment can result in a constant sense of _____, _____, and _____.

24) How would you describe a narcissist?

_____

_____

_____

_____

25) What does a narcissist do with his or her shame?

_____

_____

26) Do you know anyone who is a narcissist? If yes, how have they impacted your life?

_____

_____

_____

_____

27) How can you please a narcissist?

_____

_____

28) What will happen if you do not please a narcissist?

_____

_____

29) Why is it difficult to feel forgiven when confessing inappropriate shame to God?

_____

_____

30) If you are carrying someone else's shame, what do you need rather than forgiveness? Hint: Romans 12:1-2

_____

_____

_____

31) You need to offer yourself as a _____ _____ to God for the renewing of your mind, not offer yourself to someone else for its continued distortion.

32) As a mind continues to be renewed, it no longer _____ the inappropriate shame of others, or the toxic rules that were injected into it by unreliable rule-providers.

33) Describe healthy narcissism.

_____

_____

_____

_____

34) Do you believe that God has no problem with you enjoying your accomplishments and finding satisfaction, as long as your accomplishments and that satisfaction do not displace Him? What does godly personal satisfaction and healthy narcissism feel like?

_____

_____

35) Do you think you can develop skills for interacting with others based on the observations of your observing ego? What can you do to make your observing ego healthier?

_____

_____

36) Do you, or others, condemn you for the impact your hormones have on you? If so, how can you address this with yourself and them?

_____

_____

_____

37) Do you let your body image get in the way of physical intimacy with your spouse? If so, how can you better appreciate the fact that you are a gift to your spouse?

_____

_____

_____

38) What are your desires and needs in the area of physical intimacy? Are you content with this aspect of your relationship? If not, what would you like your spouse to know and how might the two of you begin exploring this important area?

_____

_____

_____

We Questions

39) When the two of you are arguing, are you able to participate and observe the argument without becoming immersed and losing your perspective? Is this a skill you want to develop? If not, why? What one thing could you do differently?

_____

_____

_____

_____

_____

_____

40) Do you think your arguments will decrease in frequency and intensity as the two of you develop healthier observing egos with the ability to identify and accept your own issues? How can each of you grow in identifying and accepting your own issues? How can you help your spouse?

_____

_____

_____

_____

41) Can two people contribute to a conflict that escalates into an argument without either being wrong? If so, how? When in the past has this happened in your relationship?

_____

_____

_____

42) Do you believe that a conflict can merely be a misalignment of perspectives that does not have to escalate into an argument with blame and shame? If so, what skills can you develop to keep a conflict from developing into an argument?

_____

_____

_____

43) If you consider yourselves to be an older couple, in what ways over the years have you continued to physically express your love for each other? If you have not and still want to, how will the two of you begin to reclaim God's provision to each of you from each of you?

_____

_____

_____

_____

_____

Your Thoughts

_____

_____

_____

_____

_____

_____

_____

_____

_____

_____

_____

_____

_____

_____

_____

_____

_____

_____

Subject: Re: Your Observing Ego and Shame
Main Points

Everyone can be a living squirming sacrifice who tries to get off of God's altar.

People can blame you for treating them in a negative way, such as criticizing or judging, that they do far worse to themselves with their unhealthy observing ego.

If you have an unhealthy observing ego, it can make you overly sensitive to the criticisms of others.

If you had a difficult childhood, your parents or caregivers may not have known how to love themselves, each other, or you.

Me Questions

1) Can you relate to being a living squirming sacrifice who tries to get off of God's altar? If so, what makes God's altar so uncomfortable?

   _____

   _____

2) Do you often blame others for treating you in a negative way, such as criticizing or judging, that you do far worse to yourself with your unhealthy observing ego? If so, when did you learn how to do this and who taught you?

   _____

   _____

3) Are you overly sensitive to the criticisms of others? If so, why? Have others criticized you so harshly in the past that now you have internalized their criticisms as rules in your observing ego? If so, who were/are they? How long will you let their rules remain?

   _____

   _____

4) Did your parents or caregivers know how to love themselves, each other, and you? If not, what impact has that had on you?

   _____

   _____

We Questions

5) How can you help each other offer yourselves as a living sacrifice?

_____

_____

6) How can you become less critical and judgmental of each other?

_____

_____

Your Thoughts

_____

_____

_____

_____

_____

_____

_____

_____

_____

_____

_____

_____

_____

_____

Subject: Re: Re: Your Observing Ego and Shame
Main Points

There is no *too late* with God

Parents often find Jesus and turn their lives around when their children are older. The problem is that if their children are teenagers or young adults, they have already developed most of the rules for their observing ego along with automatic instincts for survival.

Teenagers can respond with, "It's great for them, but too late for me!"

There is no "too late" with God. The rules of your observing ego and your instincts for survival can always be changed.

Psalm 51:10-12 is encouraging for your spiritual walk.

> Create in me a pure heart, O God,
>   and renew a steadfast spirit within me.
> [11] Do not cast me from your presence
>   or take your Holy Spirit from me.
> [12] Restore to me the joy of your salvation
>   and grant me a willing spirit, to sustain me. (Psalm 51:10-12)

The vast majority of parents do not wake up each morning wondering, "How can I mess my kids up even more today?"

It is difficult for parents to give what they never received and do not have.

Everyone progresses through various stages of growth that, unfortunately, may not occur soon enough for some relationships, especially relationships with their children.

Apologizing to others

Everyone makes mistakes in their relationships, and if there is a path to peace and reconciliation, it begins with accepting responsibility, offering an apology, and trying really hard not to do it again.

If you want forgiveness and mercy from those you have offended, you also must give forgiveness and mercy to those who have offended you.

When apologizing to someone, asking for forgiveness can pose a bit of a problem. It can be perceived as wanting even more from the person who was wronged.

Forgiveness should be a *freewill gift* from the person who was wronged, not words that he or she is *compelled* to speak to make the offender feel better.

One approach when asking for forgiveness is to say, "If you can forgive me I would appreciate it, and if you cannot, I understand." If someone is unwilling to forgive you, your only choice is to release it to the Holy Spirit.

Sufficient grace from God

Ultimately, when it comes to your sins and offenses toward others, you need to find the same *sufficient grace* from God for yourself that was sufficient for the Apostle Paul when he wrote in 2 Corinthians 12:9 about his request for the Lord to take away a "thorn in the flesh." The Lord's response and Paul's conclusion was,

> "'My grace is sufficient for you, for my power is made perfect in weakness.' Therefore I will boast all the more gladly about my weaknesses, so that Christ's power may rest on me."

You may not be to the point of boasting about your weaknesses, but over the years you will hopefully be able to be more and more honest about them.

Issues from the past can continue to be expressed

Many of the issues that families have had in the past are not only "in the past," but are also being expressed in the present.

Many issues from your past can still hang around and continue to be expressed through broken rules and behaviors that you now need to continually present to God for the renewing of your mind.

Renewing your mind takes time, and is why you need to be intentional with God about asking for forgiveness and continually offering yourself as a living sacrifice.

Life is a long and difficult journey with no shortcuts or easy solutions. Even so, it is doubtful that you can think of anything better to do with the time you are given.

Me Questions

1) Did your parents or caregivers find Jesus and turn their lives around after you were older? If so, do or did, you struggle with that? What impact does or did it have on you?

_____

_____

_____

_____

_____

_____

_____

_____

2) What automatic instincts for survival and rules for your observing ego were established by the time you were a teenager?

_____

_____

3) Is there no "too late" for building a healthy relationship with God? If not, why?

_____

_____

4) How can Psalm 51:10-12 be possible for you?

> Create in me a pure heart, O God,
>   and renew a steadfast spirit within me.
> [11] Do not cast me from your presence
>   or take your Holy Spirit from me.
> [12] Restore to me the joy of your salvation
>   and grant me a willing spirit, to sustain me.

_____

_____

5) What rules of your observing ego need to be rethought?

_____

_____

6) Do you believe that your parents did not wake up each morning wondering, "How can I mess my kids up even more today?" What was done right and what was done wrong?

_____

_____

_____

_____

7) Does the statement, "It is difficult for parents to give what they never received and do not have," make sense to you? What did your parents not receive from their parents and never have that you would liked to have received from them so you could give it to your children? Where else might you learn about it so you will have it to give?

_____

_____

8) Can you relate to the statement, "Everyone progresses through various stages of growth that, unfortunately, may not occur soon enough for some relationships, especially relationships with their children"? If so, in what way? Can anything be done about it? If so, what?

_____

_____

9) Is it difficult for you to accept and take responsibility for the mistakes you have made in relationships? If so, why?

_____

_____

10) Did anyone during your childhood model how to take responsibility for your mistakes? If so, who and how did they do it? If not, who can you talk with to learn how?

_____

_____

11) What do you think about the statement, "Forgiveness should be a *freewill gift* from the person who was wronged, not words that he or she is *compelled* to speak to make the offender feel better"?

_____

_____

_____

12) What do you think about the statement, "If you can forgive me I would appreciate it, and if you cannot, I understand"?

_____

_____

13) If someone is not willing to forgive you, are you able to release it to the Holy Spirit? If not, why?

_____

_____

14) What do you think about the *sufficient grace* from God that the Apostle Paul wrote about in 2 Corinthians 12:9? Is God's grace sufficient for you? If not, why?

_____

_____

_____

15) Can you think of anything better and possibly more painful to do than work on your life and marriage? What could make it painful?

_____

_____

_____

We Questions

16) Does wanting forgiveness and mercy *from each other* mean that you also must give forgiveness and mercy *to each other*? Why can that be difficult? In what ways do you do this?

_____

_____

_____

17) What childhood issues do either of you have that continue to be expressed in your marriage relationship?

_____

_____

18) Which broken rules and behaviors reinforce the expression of your childhood issues? How do those broken rules and behaviors influence your relationship?

_____

_____

19) How can the two of you continually offer your issues, rules, and behaviors to God for the renewing of your mind?

_____

_____

Your Thoughts

_____

_____

_____

_____

_____

_____

_____

_____

_____

_____

_____

Subject: Re: Arguing, Needs, Love, and Respect
Main Points

People have reasons for their thoughts and actions

People have reasons for their thoughts and actions, even when, in some cases, those thoughts and actions are self-destructive and/or hurt others.

People do whatever makes sense to them.

If you do not understand why someone does something, you probably do not have or understand enough of the pieces to their puzzle. The word "enough" is important because no one has or understands all of the pieces to anyone's puzzle, including their own.

Ask the Holy Spirit to reveal to you what you need to change, along with how and why.

It is God who helps you want to change and empowers you to do so as Paul states in Philippians.

> Therefore, my dear friends, as you have always obeyed—not only in my presence, but now much more in my absence—continue to work out your salvation with fear and trembling, 13 for it is God who works in you to will and to act in order to fulfill his good purpose. (Philippians 2:12-13)

When a couple is not living according to God's wisdom, there are consequences of their beliefs and actions to themselves and others.

Then truth and now truth

Then truth is what was true in the past, and *now truth* is what is true in the present.

It is essential for you and your spouse to create a *now truth* that is based as much as possible on evidence of love, hopeful assumptions, and fulfilled godly desires and needs.

Both husbands and wives need love and respect

The needs of you and your spouse are the same, though the intensity of each will vary between the two of you.

Both you and your spouse need love and respect.

Few people are fine without acceptance, a sense of belonging, or affirmation by others. Those who claim they are, are likely well-defended against their pain.

You and your spouse having the same needs that vary in intensity makes sense because both of you are being conformed to your unique images of the same Jesus.

Desirable traits of a wife or husband

The following paragraph describes for some what is desirable in a wife.

> I desire a peaceful, steady, and consistent wife who listens to my dreams, and believes in me. Someone who is willing to hear God equally for the two of us, and has the courage to speak the truth in love when I have lost my perspective. I need a wife who is strong, gentle, and confident that God will provide for us as we work together. I need a wife who knows me and loves me in the midst of my struggles and failures, as well as my efforts and successes. I need a wife to share it all, and celebrate the achievements with me, and mourn the losses. My wife needs to be a partner who seeks neither to dominate me nor make me her idol.

Who would prefer the opposite as follows?

> I desire an angry, chaotic, and inconsistent wife who refuses to listen to my dreams, and continually doubts me. I want someone who is willing to hear only her desires, and has the aggression to speak her criticisms when I have lost my perspective. I need a wife who is vacillating, hostile, and convinced that I am the only one who provides for us. I need a wife who does not know me and condemns me in the midst of my struggles and failures, as well as minimizes my efforts and successes. I need a wife to keep all that she wants, and who only enjoys the achievements with me, while blaming me for the losses. My wife needs to be a person who dominates me and makes me her idol when it suits her to get what she wants.

The following paragraph describes for some what is desirable in a husband.

> I desire a peaceful, steady, consistent husband who listens to my dreams and believes in me. Someone who is willing to hear God equally for the two of us, and has the courage to speak the truth in love when I have lost my perspective. I need a husband who is strong, gentle, and confident that God will provide for us as we work together. I need a husband who knows me and loves me in the midst of my struggles and failures, as well as my efforts and successes. I need a husband to share it all, and celebrate the achievements with me, and mourn the losses. My husband needs to be a partner who seeks neither to dominate me nor make me his idol.

And, here is the opposite.

> I desire an angry, chaotic, and inconsistent husband who refuses to listen to my dreams, and continually doubts me. I want someone who is willing to hear only his desires and has the aggression to speak his criticisms when I have lost my perspective. I need a husband who is

vacillating, hostile, and convinced that I am the only one who provides for us. I need a husband who does not know me and condemns me in the midst of my struggles and failures, as well as minimizes my efforts and successes. I need a husband to keep all that he wants, and who only enjoys the achievements with me, while blaming me for the losses. My husband needs to be a person who dominates me and makes me his idol when it suits him to get what he wants.

Is any wife like the positive description all the time? No. Is any husband like the positive description all the time? No. Can wives and husbands grow to become more and more like those positive descriptions by the grace and mercy of God in the power of the Holy Spirit? Absolutely!

Do not ignore your needs

You should not be preoccupied with your needs, though, you should not ignore them either.

The New International Version of Philippians 2:3-4 says,

> Do nothing out of selfish ambition or vain conceit. Rather, in humility value others above yourselves, [4] not looking to your own interests but each of you to the interests of the others.

The English Standard Version (ESV) of Philippians 2:4 says, "Let each of you look not only to his own interests, but also to the interests of others." The "not only" is important to note.

If your own needs remain unmet indefinitely, you eventually will not be able to meet any of the needs of others.

It is difficult for you to hear the Holy Spirit for others and give wise counsel when you are exhausted.

The Holy Spirit can use you when you are exhausted, but exhaustion should not be your typical state.

Your best example of someone tending to their personal needs and taking time for rest and prayer is Jesus who, "…often withdrew to lonely places and prayed" (Luke 5:16).

And, if Jesus' example is not compelling enough, even a dog with a litter of puppies knows enough to get up, shake them off when necessary, get some food and water, and take a needed stroll in the backyard. And, how those puppies (and people) will howl. She learns that everything will be fine as long as she takes care of herself enough to have something left to give.

It is true that according to Acts 20:35 it is, "…more blessed to give than to receive," but that does not mean it is not blessed to receive, just more so to give.

Someone in a relationship who is not willing to receive, denies the other the joy of giving. And, someone in a relationship who is always giving, denies the other person the opportunity to grow in that area.

To be healthy in the Body of Christ, you need to be honest with yourself and others about your needs.

Healthy relationships are give and receive

Rather than "give and take," healthy relationships are "give and receive," in that one person gives and the other receives what is offered.

People who "take" from a relationship, often end up taking more than what the giver was willing to give, even though the giver may not resist. This taking is more characteristic of fleas and intestinal parasites robbing life from a dog or cat.

Give only what you intend to give because anything beyond that will leave you feeling drained and abused. This can only occur with your permission, the result of your naïveté, or perhaps a willingness or psychological need to be abused.

Whatever you give needs to be intentional for it to be a gift.

Abuse in the area of giving and receiving can be a reenactment of childhood wounds for those whose desires and needs were not acknowledged, affirmed, and met by parents, caregivers, family members, or peers.

An observing ego's broken rule for a *give and receive* relationship can be one of *give and only give*.

Some people whose needs were not met when they were a child become takers and think the world owes them whatever they want whenever they want it.

Both the complete suppression of personal needs by one spouse, or the selfish demand that all desires be met by the other are toxic to a marriage relationship.

The following logic of a child in a stressed family makes sense at a child level. "I love my parents. My parents are sad. My needs will make them even sadder. I will keep my needs to myself. I have no needs."

Jesus often calls others to meet our needs

It is dangerous to look only to Jesus to meet your needs when He is calling someone near you to meet your needs as part of His will.

If Jesus is all we need, why do we ever feel lonely?

Jesus is there to help you endure your tragedies and pain, but He rarely makes it as though they never happened.

You and your spouse will fail at times to meet each other's needs. The important question is, "What do the two of you do after your inevitable failures?"

Healing and growth occurs in marriage when, as a couple, you address the real causes of your conflicts, which more often than not are rooted in your desires, needs, fears, wounds, defenses, and assumptions.

Self-love

Your first and foremost need from yourself is self-love because nothing good comes from self-loathing or self-condemnation.

> Hearing that Jesus had silenced the Sadducees, the Pharisees got together. [35] One of them, an expert in the law, tested him with this question: [36] "Teacher, which is the greatest commandment in the Law?"
>
> [37] Jesus replied: "'Love the Lord your God with all your heart and with all your soul and with all your mind.' [38] This is the first and greatest commandment. [39] And the second is like it: 'Love your neighbor as yourself.' [40] All the Law and the Prophets hang on these two commandments." (Matthew 22:34-40)

In this passage, Jesus explicitly gives you not only permission to love yourself, but in the second commandment, He makes it an *imperative*. You must do this in order to carry out the second greatest commandment which is to "Love your neighbor as yourself."

How can you genuinely provide for the desires and needs of your neighbors if you ignore your own?

How can you offer genuine love to your neighbors that you do not give to yourself? There is a difference between acting loving and being loving.

Self-love requires a genuine *non-condemning* and *non-condoning* belief system; not condemning your humanness, and not condoning your failures.

Everyone struggles with the discrepancy between what they want to do, compared to what they end up doing. The Apostle Paul expressed it quite clearly in Romans 7:15. " I do not understand what I do. For what I want to do I do not do, but what I hate I do."

Your desires and needs should matter to you because they matter to Jesus. They are guides not only for your healing and growth, but also for your spouse as he or she grows in the ability to respond to you.

 Jesus does not reject you because of your needs the way others often do.

It is when you accept your needs that you more fully and authentically accept yourself, along with who you are in the body of Christ, and the promise of who God will enable you to become.

You need to receive and experience the grace and mercy that Jesus suffered, died, and was resurrected to give you.

Me Questions

1) What do you think about the statement, "People have reasons for their thoughts and actions, even when, in some cases, those thoughts and actions are self-destructive and/or hurt others"?

_____

_____

2) Do you think the statement, "Rely on the Holy Spirit to reveal what needs to be changed, along with when and why" can be abused? If so, how?

_____

_____

3) Do you believe it is God who helps people want to change and empowers them to do so as Paul states in Philippians 2:12-13? What is your experience with this?

_____

_____

4) If there are harmful consequences for not living according to God's wisdom, why do you think people continue to do so?

_____

_____

5) What examples do you have of a *then truth* from your past that you still believe, but is no longer helpful in the present? What corresponding *now truth* would be helpful?

_____

_____

_____

_____

_____

6) Which of your needs should be ignored? If any, why?

_____

_____

7) Is it true that if your own needs remain unmet indefinitely, you eventually will not be able to meet any of the needs of others? How large is your deficit of unmet needs? How long can this continue?

_____

_____

8) Is it true that it is difficult to hear the Holy Spirit for others and give wise counsel when you are exhausted? What can you do to prevent yourself from becoming exhausted?

_____

_____

9) Is it true that to be healthy, you need to be honest about your needs with yourself and others? If so, why? If not, why?

_____

_____

10) What do you think about the statement, "Healthy relationships are 'give and receive,' in that one person gives and the other receives what is offered"? How is that different from "give and take?"

_____

_____

_____

_____

_____

_____

11) Who has taken more from you than you were willing to give? What was the earliest point at which you knew it was happening? Was it with your permission, the result of naïveté, or perhaps a willingness or psychological need to be abused?

_____

_____

_____

12) Was there abuse during your childhood in the area of giving and receiving in that your desires and needs were not acknowledged, affirmed, and met by parents, caregivers, family members, or peers? If so, what is the current impact of that experience on the rules of your observing ego and your behavior when it comes to giving and asking for help?

_____

_____

_____

13) Do you know people who are takers and think the world owes them whatever they want whenever they want it? What during their childhood contributed to forming this world view?

_____

_____

_____

_____

14) Do you know anyone who as a child had the logic of, "I love my parents. My parents are sad. My needs will make them sadder. I will keep my needs to myself. I have no needs"? If so, in what ways has that influenced how they relate to others?

_____

_____

_____

_____

15) What do you think about the statement, "It is dangerous to look only to Jesus to meet your needs when He is calling someone near you to meet your needs as part of His will"?

_____

_____

16) Is it true that Jesus is there to help you endure your tragedies and pain, but He rarely makes it as though they never happened? If not, why?

_____

_____

_____

17) Is it difficult for you to admit that at times you fail? If so, why? What do you do after your inevitable failures?

_____

_____

18) What do you think about the statement, "Your first and foremost need from yourself is self-love because nothing good comes from self-loathing or self-condemnation"?

_____

_____

19) Do you agree that Jesus explicitly gives you not only permission to love yourself, but He makes it an imperative in order for you to carry out the second greatest commandment, which is to love your neighbor as yourself? If not, why?

_____

_____

_____

_____

20) How can you genuinely provide for the desires and needs of your neighbors if you ignore your own? If you ignore your needs, how long can you continue to do so?

_____

_____

_____

21) How can you offer a genuine love to your neighbors that you do not give to yourself? Is it okay to merely *act* loving rather than *be* loving?

_____

_____

_____

22) In what ways do you struggle with what the Apostle Paul expressed in Romans 7:15. " I do not understand what I do. For what I want to do I do not do, but what I hate I do"?

_____

_____

_____

23) What are your thoughts on having a *non-condemning* and *non-condoning* belief system when it comes to your humanness and failures? This means to not condemn your humanness and not condone your failures.

_____

_____

24) Do your desires and needs truly matter to Jesus? If not, why do you think they don't?

_____

_____

_____

25) What do you think about the statement, "Jesus does not reject you because of your needs the way others often do"?

_____

_____

_____

26) Is it true that when you accept your needs you are more fully and authentically accepting yourself along with who you are in the body of Christ and the promise of who God will enable you to become? If so, what is the promise for who God will enable you to become? If not, why?

_____

_____

_____

_____

_____

27) Can your desires and needs serve as guides for your healing and growth as well as the healing and growth of your spouse as he or she matures in the ability to respond to you? If so, what are those desires and needs, and what responses would God honor?

_____

_____

_____

_____

_____

28) Is it difficult for you to receive and experience the grace and mercy that Jesus suffered, died, and was resurrected to give you? If so, why?

_____

_____

_____

We Questions

29) Do you believe it is essential for the two of you to create a satisfying *now truth* that is based as much as possible on hopeful assumptions, and characterized by fulfilled godly desires and needs? How would you begin doing that?

_____

_____

30) Both the complete suppression of personal needs by one spouse, or the selfish demand that all desires be met by the other are toxic to a marriage relationship. How do each of you address the needs and desires of the other?

_____

_____

31) Does it makes sense that the two of you would have the same needs because you both are being conformed to your own unique image of the same Jesus? If so, why? If not, why?

_____

_____

_____

32) How do the needs of the two of you vary in intensity?

_____

_____

_____

33) Is either of you fine with no acceptance, belonging, or affirmation? If not, what changes need to be made? How will you make them?

_____

_____

34) Is the following statement true? Healing and growth only occurs in marriage when, as a couple, both spouses address the real causes of their conflicts, which more often than not are rooted in their desires, needs, fears, wounds, defenses, and assumptions. If you do not think it is, why? If you do, how have these issues affected your marriage, and how are the two of you addressing them?

_____

_____

_____

35) How is healing and growth lived out in your relationship?

_____

_____

_____

_____

Your Thoughts

_____

_____

_____

_____

_____

_____

_____

_____

_____

_____

_____

_____

_____

Subject: Boundaries and Needs
Main Points

People assume a lot when they are trying to help others.

Talking about your desires and needs with your spouse can be helpful if the two of you are a couple and not in an abusive relationship with each other.

Spouses are not mind readers, though many times they can make a pretty accurate guess.

Your spouse is responsible for his or her own feelings and the communication of them to you. It is your responsibility to listen.

Some discomfort in your relationship is necessary for healing and growth to occur.

You and your spouse can be flawed and amazing and be completely blessed to be married to each other.

You should explore your godly desires and needs.

Exploring a desire or need with your spouse is not being selfish. However, it may be if you demand that it be met in a way that your spouse does not support.

Conflicting desires and needs between spouses are common.

Pray for insight into the possibility that even deeper and more relevant desires and needs are giving rise to those you are experiencing.

Then truth and *now truth* can apply to many areas, of which accepting Jesus as your Savior is the most important. *Then* you were not saved, and *now* you are.

Me Questions

1) What do people assume about you?

_____

_____

2) What do you assume about yourself?

_____

_____

_____

_____

3) In what ways can you explore a felt desire or need to see if it is justified?

_____

_____

4) What deeper and more relevant desires and needs could be giving rise to those you are experiencing?

_____

_____

We Questions

5) In what ways do the two of you expect each other to be a mind reader?

_____

_____

6) In what ways can each of you be responsible for communicating your feelings to the other?

_____

_____

7) Can both of you accept that some discomfort in your relationship is necessary for healing and growth to occur? What discomfort are you experiencing? How can this discomfort lead to healing and growth?

_____

_____

8) What desires and needs do the two of you have that are different from each other?

_____

_____

Your Thoughts

_____

_____

_____

_____

_____

_____

_____

_____

_____

_____

_____

_____

_____

_____

Subject: Re: Boundaries and Needs
Main Points

Your marriage is sacred ground.

Some pain in your healing and growth is necessary.

It takes courage for you to set and maintain healthy boundaries in relationships.

Speaking the truth in love

Embrace and examine your desires and needs in light of Scripture and God's wisdom.

The wisdom and rules that emerge as a result of childhood wounds are often driven by the fear of being re-wounded and rejected. Rule: *Do not tell the truth if there is a chance it will hurt someone's feelings because they will reject you.*

Childhood wisdom and rules are usually not helpful in building a healthy marriage.

Speaking the truth in love and wanting to hear the truth is not only essential for your healing and growth in a mutually satisfying marriage, it is also essential for the healthy functioning of the Body of Christ.

Us time

There are three types of *us time* found in the following passage from Ephesians.

> [14] so that we may no longer be children, tossed to and fro by the waves and carried about by every wind of doctrine, by human cunning, by craftiness in deceitful schemes. [15] Rather, speaking the truth in love, we are to grow up in every way into him who is the head, into Christ, [16] from whom the whole body, joined and held together by every joint with which it is equipped, when each part is working properly, makes the body grow so that it builds itself up in love. (Ephesians 4:14-16)

The first type of *us time* in the passage above is with you and Jesus. The second *us time* is with you and His Body of Believers. The third is with you and your spouse.

Be more intentional in seeking and leaning into your *us time* with Jesus.

Christians are partners in the Body of Christ and need quality *us time* with one another.

You and your spouse, in addition to being members of the Body of Christ, are partners in your marriage relationship and need meaningful *us time* together.

If you and your spouse are not intentional about *us time*, the two of you can become associated roommates engaged in parallel lives of functional convenience.

An efficient marriage is a poor substitute for one of intimacy.

Spouses are often unaware of their need to grow in a specific area such as *us time* in order to be more content and conformed to the image of Jesus. However, many spouses are aware and simply do not want to.

Family strengths and weaknesses

Honestly evaluating the relationship dynamics in your family of origin is not by nature being critical and judgmental. Every family has its strengths and weaknesses.

Children usually adapt to their family's strengths and weaknesses by forming rules and behaviors for either thriving or surviving.

Grow in each other's strengths

Ideally, you and your spouse bring the strengths of your family of origin to your marriage, and use your marriage to heal and grow in your weaknesses.

One spouse's desire for more *us time* with the other may be a need of which the other is not yet fully aware.

Any mismatch between you and your spouse in acknowledged or unacknowledged desires and needs will bring about conflict until those needs and desires are recognized and the mismatch either resolved or accepted.

The best path for you and your spouse is to intentionally, faithfully, and courageously speak the truth in love for the mental, emotional, spiritual, and physical health of each other and your relationship.

People often choose someone to marry who is strong in the areas that they are weak. Their choice also tends to be not as strong in their areas of strength.

The mismatch of strengths between spouses, and the opportunity for healing and growth in their weaknesses, is one of God's purposes for the well-established phenomenon, "Opposites attract."

Me Questions

1) How do you set and maintain healthy boundaries with your spouse? What are those boundaries and how are they healthy for both of you?

_____

_____

_____

_____

_____

2) How justified are your desires and needs in light of Scripture and God's wisdom?

_____

_____

3) What wisdom, rules, and instincts that you established in childhood were the result of wounds and a fear of being re-wounded and/or rejected?

_____

_____

4) Which of your childhood wisdom, rules, and instincts are not helpful in building a mutually satisfying marriage?

_____

_____

5) What strengths characterize your family of origin?

_____

_____

6) What weaknesses characterize your family of origin?

_____

_____

7) What were the most important instincts that you developed for either thriving or surviving in your family of origin? Why were they so important?

_____

_____

_____

_____

We Questions

8) In what ways is your marriage sacred ground?

_____

_____

9) What pain do the two of you experience when it comes to healing and growth in your relationship?

_____

_____

10) Do both of you have enough *us time* with each other? If not, how can you have more?

_____

_____

11) To what extent have the two of you become associated roommates who are engaged in parallel lives of functional convenience? Are you satisfied with your current state? If not, how can you be intentional about growing closer in this area?

_____

_____

12) What do you think about the statement, "An efficient marriage is a poor substitute for one of intimacy"?

_____

_____

13) What desires and needs have routinely brought about conflict in your marriage? How can each of you grow in your ability to respond to each other's desires and needs?

_____

_____

14) What do the two of you think about the statement, "The best path for you and your spouse is to intentionally, faithfully, and courageously speak the truth in love for the mental, emotional, spiritual, and physical health of each other and your relationship"? Is this always true? If not, why?

_____

_____

Your Thoughts

_____

_____

_____

_____

_____

_____

_____

_____

_____

_____

_____

_____

Subject: Opposites Attract
Main Points

Opposites attract.

It's possible to be crazy *for* your spouse, and made crazy *by* your spouse.

For questions, see next section.

Subject: Re: Opposites Attract
Main Points

Attraction of opposites is for healing and growth

Since God's will is for you to be conformed to your unique image of Jesus, he uses many types of relationships in your life to help bring this about.

The most intense, productive, and potentially destructive relationship is marriage.

One of God's purposes for the attraction of opposites is their healing and growth.

When two people of opposite strengths first find each other, they often feel like a whole human being because an area of weakness in one is covered by a strength of the other. Obviously, this is not always true, but the tendency is well established.

God wants you and your spouse to mature and grow in each other's strengths so both of you will be more fully conformed to the image of Jesus.

The strength in one spouse, serves as a model for the other to observe and build into his or her own character.

Sometimes spouses react to the other's strengths with criticism and dismissal. They view God's provision through the other with contempt.

Your spouse's desires and needs often represent areas in which God wants you to grow in order to fulfill those desires and needs.

Discomfort in your relationship often is an indicator of an area that needs healing and/or growth.

If there is no discomfort in one spouse for the lack of connection with the other, the need for growth is especially true.

The growth and development that God was unable to achieve through your family of origin and personal experiences can be continued in your marriage relationship.

Growth in your marriage relationship can occur if both of you know what is causing your discomfort, want to heal and grow, are committed to overcoming your pain, and you know what to do.

The first step each day in achieving healing and growth is for you to offer yourself to God as a living sacrifice for the renewing of your mind. (Romans 12: 1-2)

> Therefore, I urge you, brothers and sisters, in view of God's mercy, to offer your bodies as a living sacrifice, holy and pleasing to God—this is your true and proper worship. 2 Do not conform to the pattern of this world, but be transformed by the renewing of your mind. Then you will be able to test and approve what God's will is—his good, pleasing and perfect will. (Romans 12:1-2)

A more complete expression of God's character

Your strengths are part of your unique expression of God's character.

When you and your spouse honor each other's strengths, as opposed to competing for whose are superior, your children will see a combined expression of God's character that is more complete than what is possible by either of you individually.

Competing strengths and justified weaknesses

Unfortunately, many couples insist on defending their incomplete expression of God's character along with justifying their weaknesses.

Some say, "That's just the way I was made." This begs two questions, "Made by whom, God or man?" and "Are you as fully conformed to the image of Jesus as God wants you to be?"

It is much easier to criticize and devalue someone's strengths than to grow in them.

As children build their own character and observing ego, they usually choose from the character traits, rules, and approved behaviors that they observe in their parents, caregivers, and others.

Traits that attracted can become irritating

When couples do not honor each other's strengths, the very traits that were attractive when dating become irritating when married.

For example, the boyfriend who beamed when he saw his girlfriend walk into the room becomes the husband who doesn't even look up. The girlfriend who was a joy to hold during a movie, becomes a wife who gets in the way of her husband's laptop while he is working and the movie is playing in the background. Then again, she will eventually learn to occupy herself on her phone. The girlfriend who was a joy to walk with, becomes a wife who won't stop talking during a walk because she is starved for the attention she used to get when they were dating. Everything that was new and exciting becomes common and mundane.

It is a devastating path of destruction that married couples stumble down unless they remain as intentional about building a mutually satisfying marriage as they were about pursuing each other when dating.

You must build your marriage intentionally if you want it to be mutually satisfying.

Me Questions

1) What are your thoughts on the statement, "The most intense, productive, and potentially destructive relationship is marriage"?

_____

_____

_____

2) What are your thoughts on the statement, "One of God's purposes for the attraction of opposites is their healing and growth"?

_____

_____

_____

3) Do you react to your spouse's strengths with criticism and dismissal? If so, why?

_____

_____

_____

4) Do you believe God wants you to grow and mature in your spouse's strengths? If not, why?

_____

_____

_____

5) How have your experiences formed who you are? Can you change? Is there anything you want to change? If so, what?

_____

_____

6) What strength in your spouse could serve as a model for you to observe and build into
    your own character? How would you go about doing that? If you cannot think of any of
    your spouse's strengths, are you sure?

    _____

    _____

7) What are your thoughts on the statement, "The growth and development that God was
    unable to achieve in you through your family of origin and personal experiences can be
    continued in your marriage relationship"?

    _____

    _____

8) If your strengths are your unique expression of God's character, what aspects of His
    character do you portray?

    _____

    _____

9) As children build their own character and observing ego, they usually choose from the
    character traits, rules, and approved behaviors they observe in their parents, caregivers,
    and others. Which of your character traits, rules, and approved behaviors do you want
    your children to build into their character?

    _____

    _____

We Questions

10) What traits did each of you have that were attractive when dating, but now have become
    less so when married? What has changed?

    _____

    _____

    _____

11) For each of you, what are your strengths and weaknesses? Have you been able to acknowledge and yield to each other's strengths as God's provision to you? If not, why?

_____

_____

_____

12) Do the two of you insist on defending your incomplete expressions of God's character, along with justifying your weaknesses? If so, why?

_____

_____

_____

13) Growth in your marriage relationship can only occur if you and your spouse know what is causing your discomfort, want to heal and grow, are committed to overcoming the pain, and know what to do. How are the two of you doing in these four areas?

_____

_____

_____

14) What of God's character does someone see when they look at your combined strengths?

_____

_____

_____

15) How are the two of you intentionally building a personally and mutually satisfying marriage?

_____

_____

_____

_____

Your Thoughts

_____

_____

_____

_____

_____

_____

_____

_____

_____

_____

_____

_____

_____

_____

_____

_____

_____

_____

_____

_____

_____

_____

_____

Subject: Re: Re: Opposites Attract
Main Points

There is nothing wrong with you and your spouse having a unique representation of the image of Jesus.

Opposite strengths in your relationship with your spouse and others is God's design.

Conforming to win the approval of others does not result in being conformed to the image of Jesus.

Me Questions

1) Do you find it unsettling that your spouse can have a unique representation of the image of Jesus that is different from yours? If so, why?

_____

_____

_____

_____

2) What are your thoughts on the statement, "The opposite strengths of you and your spouse are God's design for your marriage.

_____

_____

_____

_____

We Question

3) What are your opposite strengths and how do you integrate them in your marriage?

_____

_____

_____

Your Thoughts

_____
_____
_____
_____
_____
_____
_____
_____
_____
_____
_____
_____
_____
_____
_____

Subject: Fix or Facilitate
Main Points

Anything you try to improve in your relationship may not work the first time.

Answer Mode
Do not immediately and without invitation go into Answer Mode with your spouse.

Be genuinely curious
Rather than try to fix your spouse's problem with an answer, your role is to facilitate your spouse in understanding what he or she thinks and feels, and in becoming a better problem-solver.

When your spouse is trying to help you by asking meaningful questions, be willing to honestly explore your thoughts and feelings.

Be genuinely curious about your spouse's situation and ask questions. These questions follow the pattern of Who, What, When, Where, Why, and How much?

Your spouse may not have a readily available and accurate answer to the question, "Why?"

Be faithful in speaking the truth to your spouse and asking questions in love.

The purpose of asking questions is to help your spouse disentangle jumbled thoughts, and surface underlying feelings such as, fear, frustration, anxiety, and/or anger.

These questions include:

What options are you considering? (For each option that is being considered ask the following questions)

What do you like about it?

What do you not like about it?

What are the potential gains? How likely are they?

What are the potential losses? How likely are they?

How do you feel about this option? When have you felt this way before?

Do you have enough information to make a decision? If not, is there anyone you can contact who does?

Is there any way I can help?

When a question is answered, it is good to follow with, "If I understand you correctly, you are saying <repeat back>." This allows your spouse to hear his or her thoughts coming back from you, which usually results in greater clarity.

It can also be helpful to follow up an answer with, "Is there more to that?" This gives your spouse a chance to explore the possibility that there could be deeper thoughts and feelings to consider.

Asking questions and repeating back will seem mechanical at first, and perhaps even contrived, which is fine. Developing a new skill takes practice.

It is important to remember that all changes in your relationship will be clumsy at first.

Questions not to ask are:

>   Why haven't you tried <add your solution here>?
>
>   Why have you waited until now?
>
>   What do you expect me to do?
>
>   How did you get into this?
>
>   What were you thinking?
>
>   Why does this always happen to you?

These questions are, more often than not, no more than statements of condemnation, shame, and guilt hurled at someone who is already hurting.

It isn't that these questions should never be asked, it's just a matter of when the timing is right, and how they can be asked in a more effective form that will result in productive answers, healing, and growth.

Helpful alternatives to the previous questions are:

>   Are there other solutions you have thought of?
>
>   What time pressures are you under?
>
>   What can I do to be helpful?
>
>   What unforeseen events have contributed to this problem?
>
>   What logic led you to make that decision?
>
>   What do you think is contributing to this pattern?

If your spouse tends to be a fixer, you may have to say in the middle of a discussion, "Wait a minute, I'm not looking for an answer. I just need help thinking this through." Or, you may even start a discussion with the statement, "I need to talk about something and I am not looking for an answer…yet."

When your spouse is struggling with a decision, your goal should not be to *convince* him or her of your thoughts and feelings, rather, it should be first to help your spouse *understand his or her own* thoughts and feelings. Then you can speak *your truth* in love into your spouse's life.

Your truth in love

No one has the whole truth and nothing but the truth because the only *true truth* is God's truth from His perspective.

Always let love and respect prevail.

All patterns from the past are not bad

When you find yourself struggling in your relationship with your spouse, all of the previous patterns in your relationship are not bad. It is fine to return to saying and doing those things that were successful and meaningful to both of you when you were dating and first married.

Me Questions

1) How often do you go into Answer Mode with your spouse? When you do, is it helpful?

    _____

    _____

2) Describe how you would facilitate your spouse in understanding what he or she thinks and feels, and in becoming a better problem-solver.

    _____

    _____

3) Describe how you can be genuinely curious about your spouse's situation and ask questions.

    _____

    _____

4) Why can it be difficult to honestly explore yours and your spouse's thoughts and feelings?

    _____

    _____

5) Why is it important to follow your spouse's answer to a question with, "If I understand you correctly, you are saying <repeat back>"?

_____

_____

_____

6) Why is it important to follow your spouse's answer to a question with, "Is there more to that?"

_____

_____

_____

7) Rather than seeking first to understand your spouse's thoughts and feelings, how often do you find yourself trying to convince him or her about what you think and feel? How can you do better?

_____

_____

_____

8) What are your thoughts on the statement, "No one has the whole truth and nothing but the truth because the only *true truth* is God's truth from His perspective"?

_____

_____

_____

9) Why can it be so difficult to let love and respect prevail?

_____

_____

_____

We Questions

10) Are the two of you comfortable with the fact that all change will seem mechanical and clumsy at first? What changes do the two of you want to make?

_____

_____

_____

_____

11) If either of you goes into Answer Mode, is it okay for the other to say, "Wait a minute, I'm not looking for an answer. I just need help thinking this through"? If not, why?

_____

_____

_____

_____

12) Do you both feel comfortable starting a discussion with the statement, "I need to talk about something and I am not looking for an answer…yet"? If not, why?

_____

_____

_____

13) What previous patterns of interacting with each other were successful and meaningful to you both when you were dating and first married? What did you say and do? What do you have to lose by saying and doing them again?

_____

_____

_____

_____

_____

Your Thoughts

_____

_____

_____

_____

_____

_____

_____

_____

_____

_____

_____

_____

_____

_____

_____

_____

_____

_____

_____

_____

Subject: Re: Fix or Facilitate
Main Points

Keep your relationship tools ready in your mind, or on the refrigerator door.

You are human and you will fail from time to time despite your best efforts.

Me Questions

1) What relationship tools do you have ready in your mind for when you need them?

_____

_____

2) Is it okay for your spouse to fail from time to time despite his or her best efforts? If not, why?

_____

_____

We Question

3) In what ways can the two of you be intentional in building a mutually satisfying marriage?

_____

_____

Your Thoughts

_____

_____

_____

_____

_____

_____

_____

_____

_____

_____

_____

_____

_____

_____

_____

_____

_____

Subject: Pre-Fall Marriage
Main Points

Arguments and backbiting can siphon an enormous amount of energy away from a ministry, or family.

Spending time or investing in others

Invest in your spouse and others.

Begin your investing by offering yourself as a living sacrifice.

> Therefore, I urge you, brothers and sisters, in view of God's mercy, to offer your bodies as a living sacrifice, holy and pleasing to God—this is your true and proper worship. [2] Do not conform to the pattern of this world, but be transformed by the renewing of your mind. Then you will be able to test and approve what God's will is—his good, pleasing and perfect will. (Romans 12:1-2)

You can either *go to* God's altar to pray, or *climb up onto* His altar and offer yourself to Him as a *living* sacrifice.

Offering yourself is what pleases God and allows Him to not only address the ways you have become conformed to this world, but also to transform you by the renewing of your mind.

God does not want you *working for Him*, rather, He wants to *work through you*.

First century Roman culture model of marriage

First century Roman culture is not a suitable model for marriage because it emerged from a period in our Christian history when wives were considered to be the property of their husband.

Proverbs 31 model of marriage

Another model for marriage is found at the end of the Book of Proverbs 31, in which a wife does it all to the point that, "Her husband is respected at the city gate, where he takes his seat among the elders of the land." (verse 23) It isn't clear in what ways she is submitted to her husband or silent, but his job of being a husband is pretty easy given her initiative and effectiveness.

Pre-Fall model of marriage

Note: Rick and Georgeann first heard of a Pre-Fall perspective on marriage during a presentation by Steve and Katie Helgeson at Harvest Vineyard Church in Ames, Iowa.

A Pre-Fall model of marriage represents God's original will for Adam and Eve before they were banished from the Garden of Eden.

In the Sermon on the Mount Jesus taught what has become known as the Lord's Prayer.

"This, then, is how you should pray:

"'Our Father in heaven, hallowed be your name,
¹⁰ your kingdom come, your will be done,
    on earth as it is in heaven.
¹¹ Give us today our daily bread.
¹² And forgive us our debts,
    as we also have forgiven our debtors.
¹³ And lead us not into temptation,
    but deliver us from the evil one.' (Matthew 6:9-13)

When Jesus said, "your will be done on earth as it is in heaven" it is safe to assume He meant it literally.

So, what is God's will for how marriage should be done on earth? The obvious answer is in the way He created Adam and Eve to be together before the Fall.

Before the Fall, in the first account of creation God said,

> ²⁶ ..."Let us make mankind in our image, in our likeness, so that they may rule over the fish in the sea and the birds in the sky, over the livestock and all the wild animals, and over all the creatures that move along the ground." ²⁷ So God created mankind in his own image, in the image of God he created them; male and female he created them.
>
> ²⁸ God blessed them and said to them, "Be fruitful and increase in number; fill the earth and subdue it. Rule over the fish in the sea and the birds in the sky and over every living creature that moves on the ground."
>
> ²⁹ Then God said, "I give you every seed-bearing plant on the face of the whole earth and every tree that has fruit with seed in it. They will be yours for food. ³⁰ And to all the beasts of the earth and all the birds in the sky and all the creatures that move along the ground—everything that has the breath of life in it—I give every green plant for food." And it was so.
>
> ³¹ God saw all that he had made, and it was very good. And there was evening, and there was morning—the sixth day. (Genesis 1:26-31)

When God said, "Let us make mankind in our image, in our likeness so that they may rule…" it gives a sense of the beauty, love, and power that was built into "mankind" as the image of the "us" who were present at creation.

God's purpose for mankind was to "rule over the fish in the sea and the birds in the sky, over the livestock and all the wild animals, and over all the creatures that move along the ground."

Who was the "mankind" that was supposed to rule? Verse 27 says, "So God created mankind in his own image, in the image of God he created them; male and female he created them."

There is no indication that God's original will was for males to *rule over* the animals and females not to do the same. And, there is certainly no indication that God originally intended males to rule over females.

God made Adam and Eve coequal partners without a hierarchy or a distinction of dominance.

Adam and Eve were originally created to be complementary to each other, and Eve was not created to be Adam's assistant.

Together, in Adam and Eve's oneness, they reflected a greater fullness and representation of God than either could individually.

In the second account of creation in Genesis Chapter 2:18 God said, "It is not good for the man to be alone. I will make a helper suitable for him." This means that Adam was lonely, and evidently, God was not enough.

Therefore, God created Eve to make Adam complete, who also made Eve complete with Adam.

The notion of Adam ruling over Eve only surfaces after the Fall in Genesis 3:16 when God was speaking to them. '"To the woman he said, "I will make your pains in childbearing very severe; with painful labor you will give birth to children. Your desire will be for your husband, and he will rule over you."'

Some might ask, "What about what the Law says about marriage?" Or say, "We live in a fallen world, husbands rule over their wives, and that's just how it is."

First, Jesus fulfills the law as written in Matthew 5:17. "Do not think that I have come to abolish the Law or the Prophets; I have not come to abolish them but to fulfill them."

Second, as far as a fallen world is concerned, even though Christians live *in it,* they do not have to be *of it.*

If you are married and want to bring about God's will on the earth as it is in heaven, your marriage is the best place to start.

Some husbands really like the idea of ruling over their wife. These one-sided relationships are particularly endemic with Christian abusive husbands whose entire *Own Testament* consists of a single corrupted verse,

> "Wives, submit yourselves to your husbands. The wife does not have authority over her own body, but yields it to her husband. Do not deprive each other. And if she divorces her husband and marries another man, she commits adultery." (All About Me 1:1)

For a man who opts for a Post-Fall marriage, the Proverbs 31 woman is preferred over a wife aligned with first century Roman culture because it will require a lot less work on his part.

Proverbs 31 does start, however, with the question, "A wife of noble character who can find?" For the man who does find a Proverbs 31 wife, he would do well to appreciate, encourage, and praise her, rather than criticize, discourage, and condemn, which often happens when his ego feels dwarfed by her excellence.

When it comes to caring for a Proverbs 31 wife, we can learn at least one lesson from a dairy farmer. No matter how angry he gets, he is smart enough not to kick his best cow in the udder.

Me Questions

1. How does a Pre-Fall marriage differ from one based on First century Roman culture?

    _____

    _____

    _____

2. What is today's equivalent of a Proverbs 31 wife? Is this a reasonable expectation?

    _____

    _____

3. What are your thoughts on the following?

    When it comes to caring for a Proverbs 31 wife, we can learn at least one lesson from a dairy farmer. No matter how angry he gets, he is smart enough not to kick his best cow in the udder.

    _____

    _____

We Questions

4. Does a Pre-Fall marriage differ from how the two of you view marriage? If so, in what ways?

    _____

    _____

    _____

5. What do you think about the following corrupted verse?

    "Wives, submit yourselves to your husbands. The wife does not have authority over her own body, but yields it to her husband. Do not deprive each other. And if she divorces her husband and marries another man, she commits adultery." (All About Me 1:1)

    _____

    _____

    _____

    _____

6. How well do you appreciate, encourage, and praise each other? How can you do better?

    _____

    _____

    _____

    _____

7. How often do you criticize, discourage, and condemn each other? If you frequently do, why? What can you do differently?

    _____

    _____

    _____

    _____

Your Thoughts

_____

_____

_____

_____

_____

_____

_____

_____

_____

_____

_____

_____

_____

_____

_____

_____

_____

Subject: Pre-Fall Marriage and Opposites Attract
Main Points

How you feel about your spouse and yourself changes over time.

A spouse can influence how *you* feel about *yourself*.

It is important to praise without attaching a big "but." For example, "You did a good job, but if you had <fill in the criticism here>, it would have been even better.

It is important as a spouse to feel *good* enough.

Feeling attacked does not mean you are being attacked.

Withdrawing from your spouse when angry can activate his or her childhood wound of abandonment. Though, at times and for a specific period, it may be better to withdraw from your spouse than to fight and re-wound her or him.

It takes time and intentionality to connect with each other.

Sometimes a spouse just wants to be held.

Check in regularly with your spouse to see if he or she needs to talk.

If you have enough time to argue, you have enough time to talk.

A spouse can feel like he or she is carrying everything alone.

Be intentional about being the spouse God wants you to be.

Be safe with each other and communicate about your struggles, insecurities, dreams, life, and God.

Synchronizing schedules with your spouse is not connecting.

Your environment and relationships can introduce new problems with your spouse, or bring existing ones to the surface.

Distractions such as friends, work, or children can get in the way of you and your spouse dealing with marriage relationship problems.

Circumstances rarely turn out the way you think they will.

What appears to be love and acceptance when dating can be no more than placing the other person up on a pedestal.

Me Questions

1. How do you feel about yourself when you are with your spouse?

   _____

   _____

2. When your spouse praises you, is there a big "but" attached to it? If so, why do you think that is the case?

_____

_____

3. Do you feel good enough for your spouse? If not, how much of that is due to how your spouse views you? How much of it is due to how you view yourself?

_____

_____

4. What do you think about the statement, "Feeling attacked does not mean you are being attacked"?

_____

_____

5. What can you do to be more intentional about being the spouse God wants you to be?

_____

_____

6. What do you think about the statement, "Circumstances rarely turn out the way you think they will"? How often do circumstances turn out exactly the way you thought they would? When they do not, what is an appropriate response?

_____

_____

We Questions

7. What do you think about the statement, "It takes time and intentionality to connect"?

_____

_____

8. Do the two of you take the time to intentionally connect? How can you do better?

_____

_____

9. What does it mean when your spouse just wants to be held? Is that difficult for the two of you to do? If so, why?

_____

_____

10. How important is it to check in with each other regularly to see if either of you needs to talk? If you have enough time to argue, you have enough time to talk.

_____

_____

11. How can you share each other's burdens so neither of you feels like you are carrying your responsibilities alone?

_____

_____

12. Are the two of you able to be safe with each other and communicate about your struggles, insecurities, dreams, life, and God? If not, why? How can you do better?

_____

_____

13. What do you think about the statement, "Synchronizing schedules is not connecting"?

_____

_____

_____

14. How have current circumstances in your environment introduced new problems or brought existing problems to the surface? What is your plan for addressing them? Is grace and mercy part of that plan? How can the two of you respond to them?

_____

_____

_____

_____

_____

_____

15. Do you let distractions such as friends, work, or children get in the way of addressing your marriage relationship problems? If so, why? Are you avoiding your problems? If so, why? How can you do better?

_____

_____

16. Do you place each other up on a pedestal or in a pit? If so, why?

_____

_____

Your Thoughts

_____

_____

_____

_____

_____

_____

_____

_____

Subject: Good News
Main Points

Return to the caring thoughts and behaviors that you enjoyed when you were dating.

If God can raise Jesus from the dead, He can raise you, your spouse, and your marriage to the life they were meant to have.

Me Question

1. Do you think it is possible for God to raise your marriage to the life it was meant to have? If so, how can you grow in your desire, courage, and willingness to do the hard work that it requires?

_____

_____

We Question

2. If God raised your marriage to the life He intended, what would it look like? How would the two of you be different?

_____

_____

Your Thoughts

_____

_____

_____

_____

_____

_____

_____

_____

Subject: Re: Good News

Main Points

Building a mutually satisfying marriage requires intentionality from both you and your spouse.

Find ways to let your spouse know you are thinking loving thoughts about him or her when he or she is not around. Notes and cards are a good way to do this.

Openness takes time, practice, and trust.

Helping other couples

In relationships there will always be a mismatch between spouses regarding the speed and depth that they want to go into their desires, needs, fears, wounds, defenses and assumptions. What matters is how great the mismatch and in what areas. The real problem is when spouses don't want to go to the same depth, nor talk about the same issues.

Couples who are successful, patiently respect each other's process for healing and growth. When both you and your spouse are sincere and loving, time is on your side.

People who are struggling with mental illness, a personality disorder, or require medication to function will need to have help from professionals such as a licensed counselor, pastor, physician, and/or a psychiatrist.

When working with another couple, if you think you may be in over your head, then you probably are.

In an abusive relationship, the dominating person almost always does not want to be honest, while the other does.

Unfortunately, what can happen with honesty is that the spouse who is being abused feels safe when meeting with a pastor or counselor and may be brutally honest. While this is happening the abuser may act passive and accommodating, only to be brutal on the drive home and the days that follow.

You can only help a couple if both spouses want your help.

For those couples you can help, your impact on their lives, and the lives of their children and others will last for generations.

There are not enough trained counselors to meet the needs of all couples who are struggling, which means laypeople must help whenever they can. All of us can learn from one another.

Me Questions

1. In what ways do you let your spouse know you are thinking loving thoughts about him or her when he or she is not around?

    _____

    _____

2. What are your thoughts on the statement, "Openness takes time, practice, and trust"?

    _____

    _____

3. Should you and/or your spouse be on medication, or have your medication adjusted? If so, who do you need to contact and how soon can you get an appointment?

    _____

    _____

    _____

4. What do you think about the statement, "People can learn from one another"? What are the rewards and risks?

    _____

    _____

    _____

We Questions

5. How are the two of you being intentional in building a mutually satisfying marriage?

    _____

    _____

    _____

    _____

6. How evenly matched are the two of you in your commitment to understanding each other's desires, needs, fears, wounds, defenses, and assumptions? What are your areas of mismatch?

_____

_____

_____

7. Do both of you want to be honest about your relationship with yourselves and with others? If not, why?

_____

_____

_____

8. Is it safe for both of you to be honest with each other without fear of reprisal or abuse? If not, make it so. If you want a mutually satisfying marriage you must be safe with each other.

_____

_____

9. Do either of you need to seek help from a professional such as a licensed counselor, pastor, physician, and/or a psychiatrist?

_____

_____

Your Thoughts

_____

_____

_____

_____

_____

_____

_____

_____

_____

_____

_____

_____

_____

_____

_____

_____

_____

_____

Subject: Imago, Romance, Power Struggle, and a Conscious Marriage
Main Points

Decision-making
Once you and your spouse commit to an action, try not to express resistance, reluctance, second guessing, back-biting, or bitterness.

You and your spouse are human and have the right to feel what you feel, and sometimes a feeling just pops out.

If a decision that you and your spouse agreed upon does not turn out well, do not persecute the one who made the decision; your spouse or yourself.

What goes around comes around
If grace and mercy are given, they will hopefully be received in return.

Three phases of a marriage relationship
Note: What follows is heavily influenced by the work of Drs. Harville Hendrix and Helen LaKelly Hunt. Their thinking, and our own, is much more expansive and nuanced than what is included here, so please bear in mind that this explanation is an oversimplification of both. We will present three phases of the marriage relationship from Harville and Helen's work, though we are giving thought to other phases that couples may go through.

Romance phase
The romance phase of dating has so little to do with reality it could be referred to as psychosis.

During the romance phase, people tend to hide their undesirable character traits, and pretend they are the ideal match. They also tend to ignore or not perceive warning signs about the other person.

Imago
Harville Hendrix and Helen LaKelly Hunt teach that during childhood we build a subconscious image in our minds of the person who we think will be the ideal nurturing other. This image, an Imago, is derived from relationships with our parents, caregivers, siblings, and any other people who were or are influential in our life; pleasant and not so.

When someone comes along who subconsciously triggers a match with our Imago, we think the long-awaited caregiver has finally arrived who will meet all desires and needs, and will be safe and playful. Conversely, the other person is also watching for the same type of match with his or her Imago.

For example, a young woman who is treated with respect by her father or other influential person will likely be attracted to someone who does the same if her

Imago was formed around the value of respect.

Unfortunately, if she is treated with disrespect, she may be attracted to the same kind of relationship because it feels familiar. And, it is familiar because her Imago and personality were formed around that disrespectful attitude and behavior.

When couples say, "When we first met we felt like we had known each other forever." Guess what? They had, just in different people.

An Imago can also be the opposite of what someone grew up with. A woman who grew up in an environment of disrespect may have zero tolerance for the same in her other relationships.

Behaviors in a marriage relationship often mimic those in previous relationships.

A paradoxical desire and need of some people is to maintain the appearance of having no desires or needs. One reason for this can be that the psychological pain of having desires and needs that remain unmet, is more painful than pretending to have no desires or needs at all…at least for a while.

Opposites attract

Your Imago can be influenced by the phenomenon that opposites attract.

Sometimes a person who feels deeply, and values communication, is attracted to someone who is all but unaware of his or her feelings, and is barely verbal.

Power struggle

The romance phase gives way to the power struggle, in which one or both people shift from appearing to have no needs, and being desirable, to focusing on getting their desires and needs met. Agendas that were hidden come to the surface.

Tactics of the power struggle can range from pleading and passive-aggressiveness to mental, emotional, spiritual, and even physical abuse.

The focus becomes the other person's perceived inadequacies that are frequently and loudly proclaimed, without regard for one's own inadequacies.

Some spouses think screaming, pouting, or hitting will convince the other to become more nurturing, safer, playful, and more willing to fulfill childhood and current desires and needs. These are strategies used most often unsuccessfully by small children.

The power struggle is the stage when feelings of not getting what was bargained for can start up in both spouses.

Many people fall in love with their own fabricated image; their Imago, that they project onto their future spouse. What is seen is not the reality of the person. It is like projecting a movie onto a screen and thinking the images on the screen are truly part of the screen. The traits they thought they perceived were never there.

During the power struggle, negative traits that were missed become clearly visible. Sadly, these negative traits in one's spouse were often seen clearly by family and friends before the marriage.

Some intentional deceptions by a spouse during the romance phase are no more than calculated strategies used by a hunter on a hunt, and are revealed without shame once the marriage is finalized.

These hunters are content with the power struggle because they have no intention of building a *mutually* satisfying marriage.

Some spouses think a marriage certificate is the same as a car title. Once received, the holder can legally do with the other whatever he or she pleases because "God hates divorce." Recall the first century Roman culture ownership model of marriage.

Conscious marriage

Couples who emerge from the power struggle phase enter a conscious marriage where they are intentional in trying to build a mutually satisfying marriage.

The alternatives to entering into a conscious marriage are to remain in the power struggle indefinitely, or divorce and find another person with whom to go through yet another romance phase followed by the obligatory power struggle. This cycle of dead-end new beginnings can be endless; especially when someone is addicted to the hopes and emotions of the romance phase.

In a conscious marriage, reactions are replaced with responses, and couples interact in ways that promote understanding, healing, and growth.

Decades of instinctive reactions are difficult to overcome, and subduing them takes slightly longer than a lifetime.

The battle of transforming instinctive reactions into intentional responses is a power struggle that God desires for you to enter into by first offering yourself to Him as a living sacrifice. He is the one who renews your mind and conforms you to the image of his Son.

Rage towards your spouse can indicate the presence of a childhood wound.

It can be your inner-child who responds with contentment when your spouse is accepting and encouraging toward you, and it can be that same inner-child who reacts with anger when you feel rejected or ignored.

Some people are so wounded in the area of rejection or neglect they no longer feel the pain.

The inability to feel pain does not mean it is not present and does not impact the mind, emotions, spirit, and body. It just means that it is no longer perceived.

Experiencing pain when spouses withdraw from each other is good because it motivates them to get back together.

It is tragic when spouses do not have a clue how to deal with each other's desires, needs, fears, wounds, defenses, and assumptions, or one or both are too fatigued or unwilling to do so.

A common defense against experiencing the pain of abandonment and loneliness is to convert it to anger or even rage. The reason often is that experiencing anger is much more tolerable than feeling vulnerable and abandoned.

Connection to one degree or another is a required nutrient in most people's emotional diet.

One spouse should not be expected to do all of the heavy lifting when it comes to pursuing the other and trying to bring growth to the relationship.

The pursuing of each other that makes for happy dating and romance is also required for a happy and romantic mutually satisfying marriage.

Spouses can divert their need for connection with each other towards friends, work, children, or even a ministry. Such diversions at best are precursors to parallel lives, and at worst, landmarks on the road to divorce.

Of course, the other diversion is having other lovers. These relationships often begin with a mental and emotional connection that leads to a romance phase with its addictive psychosis. When the psychosis clears, however, a substitute diversion must be found to take its place.

The romance phase of a relationship must end for spouses to transition through the power struggle to a conscious marriage. It is in a conscious marriage that spouses will heal and grow with an even deeper and more abiding passion for romance, oneness, and wholeness than was possible during the romance phase.

The struggles that spouses go through are an unavoidable part of their journey to a mutually satisfying marriage.

God's perfect path is often painful.

If you are interested in learning more about Harville and Helen's work, we recommend the book, *Getting the Love You Want: A Guide for Couples* by Harville Hendrix, along with their communication initiative called, *Safe Conversations*.

Me Questions

1. Which individuals had a significant influence on the development of your Imago?

    _____

    _____

    _____

2. What are the characteristics of an ideal nurturing spouse?

    _____

    _____

    _____

    _____

3. Which of your behaviors from previous relationships are mimicked in your marriage relationship?

    _____

    _____

    _____

4. Is it difficult for you to let others know of your desires and needs? If so, why?

    _____

    _____

    _____

5. Do you expect your spouse and everyone else to meet all of your desires and needs? If so, why?

    _____

    _____

    _____

6. Do you think passive-aggressiveness, screaming, pouting, or hitting will convince your spouse to be more nurturing, safer, playful, and more willing to meet your desires and needs? If so, how often has that strategy been successful?

_____

_____

_____

7. How much of your Imago did you project onto your spouse that turned out not to be true?

_____

_____

8. Do you act like a marriage certificate is a title of ownership? If so, is that a good long-term strategy for building a mutually satisfying marriage?

_____

_____

9. Are you aware of any of your childhood wounds and instinctive reactions? If so, what are they and how do they get in the way of building a conscious marriage?

_____

_____

_____

_____

10. Have you been so wounded in the area of rejection or neglect that you no longer feel the pain? If so, how can you begin to feel again?

_____

_____

11. Do you need and value mental and emotional connection with your spouse? If not, what is your plan for building a mutually satisfying marriage?

_____

_____

_____

12. When your spouse withdraws from you, how do you feel? How old emotionally do you feel?

_____

_____

_____

13. When your spouse presses in emotionally to connect with you, how do you feel? How old emotionally do you feel?

_____

_____

_____

14. Are you too fatigued or unwilling to work on your marriage? If so, what is your plan for moving forward?

_____

_____

_____

15. Do you convert your emotions to anger? If so, with which emotions do you do that?

_____

_____

_____

We Questions

16. If a decision that one of you made does not turn out well, does the other persecute the decision maker for being wrong? If so, how helpful is that?

_____

_____

_____

17. How well do the two of you show grace and mercy to each other? If it is difficult to do so, why?

_____

_____

18. Describe the romance phase of your relationship.

_____

_____

_____

19. Describe the power struggle phase of your relationship.

_____

_____

20. What tactics do each of you use when you are in the power struggle?

_____

_____

_____

_____

_____

21. When in the power struggle, how much focus is on the other person's perceived inadequacies without regard for one's own inadequacies?

_____

_____

22. How much time and effort do the two of you invest in your conscious marriage by being intentional in what you say and do?

_____

_____

23. How much time and effort do you spend reacting to each other, rather than, responding in ways that promote understanding, healing, and growth? How can you do better?

_____

_____

_____

24. Does one of you do most of the heavy lifting when it comes to pursuing the other for mental and emotional connection, and in trying to bring growth to the relationship? If so, how can the two of you achieve a better balance?

_____

_____

_____

_____

25. What do you think about the statement, "The pursuing that makes for happy dating and romance is also required for a happy and romantic mutually satisfying marriage"?

_____

_____

_____

26. Do either or both of you divert your need for connection with each other towards your friends, work, children, or even a ministry? If so, how can that be changed? Remember, such diversions at best are precursors to parallel lives, and at worst, landmarks on the road to divorce.

_____

_____

Your Thoughts

_____

_____

_____

_____

_____

_____

_____

_____

_____

_____

_____

_____

_____

Subject: Areas of Responsibility and Physical Intimacy
Main Points

Areas of responsibility

Stay connected with your spouse and communicate in your areas of responsibility.

Shared decision-making combines the gifts that God has given to both of you.

Some arguments can be avoided by being patient and letting circumstances unfold.

Only, never, and always

Using words like *only, never,* and *always* during an argument can be distracting when you and your spouse are trying to grow closer.

When arguing it is easy to get sidetracked with comebacks that use the words only, never, and always.

For example, if your spouse says, "You only approach me when you want sex," it is not helpful to react with, "*Only*?! You mean I *never* approach you for any other reason than for sex?! It is *always* for sex?!"

It isn't about whether or not *only, never,* or *always* are always true; it just feels that way at the time those words are used. It is more helpful to look past those words in an effort to understand what your spouse is feeling and trying to say.

Physical intimacy

Physical intimacy does not have to be orgasm-focused.

Physical intimacy should be mutually satisfying and not an obligatory duty.

If sexual intimacy is desired in general, but not with your spouse, the obvious questions are, "What is missing from your relationship that has causes that desire to be lacking? And, how can that desire be rekindled?"

The intense passion of premarital sex is often a substitute for building a mentally, emotionally, spiritually, and physically healthy relationship.

Marriage is a single step on a lifelong journey to wholeness and oneness. It begins best by building a conscious relationship before getting married that is continued with building a conscious marriage after.

Acceptance and personal value

Riding the rollercoaster of acceptance by others seems fine when it is going up emotionally and you feel valued, but when that acceptance is temporarily or permanently removed, you have no choice but to ride it down and feel worthless.

You can only see your true value when you see yourself through God's eyes, which is revealed by the fact that Jesus died for you, and the Holy Spirit chooses to live in and work through you.

It is fine for you and your spouse to feel emotionally fulfilled when you are connected; though neither of you should link your feelings of personal value and self-acceptance to being accepted by the other. You and your spouse should not have that power over each other.

The saying, "Beauty is in the eye of the beholder" is fine as long as the eye is God's.

Me Questions

1. Was getting married something you did not anticipate as being a single step on a lifelong journey to wholeness and relationship oneness? If so, the reality is that now you are on that journey. What can make your journey more enjoyable and satisfying?

   _____

   _____

   _____

   _____

2. If physical intimacy is desired in general, but not with your spouse, "What is missing from your relationship?" If what is missing was there in the past, what changed and why?

   _____

   _____

   _____

   _____

3. Do you value yourself based on the acceptance of others? If so, are you comfortable being that vulnerable by giving them power over you? How can you take back your power?

   _____

   _____

   _____

   _____

4. How do you think God really sees you through His eyes? Are you worthy of the blood of Jesus and the working of the Holy Spirit in you?

_____

_____

_____

5. What are your thoughts on the following statement. "The saying, 'Beauty is in the eye of the beholder' is fine as long as the eye is God's"?

_____

_____

We Questions

6. How well do the two of you share decision-making by combining the gifts that God has given to each of you?

_____

_____

_____

7. What are your thoughts on the statement, "Some arguments can be avoided by being patient and letting circumstances unfold"? Are you both able to do this? How can this cause problems?

_____

_____

_____

8. When arguing, how often do the two of you get hung up on words like *only*, *never*, and *always*? How can the two of you do better?

_____

_____

9. Does physical intimacy for the two of you have to be orgasm-focused? If yes, is that mutually satisfying? If no, is that mutually satisfying? How can you be more intimate?

    _____

    _____

10. Is physical intimacy considered to be an obligatory duty by one of you? If so, how can this be experienced differently?

    _____

    _____

11. Did the two of you use premarital sex as a substitute for building a mentally, emotionally, spiritually, and physically healthy relationship? If so, it is not too late to do the work to correct that. What first steps can the two of you take together?

    _____

    _____

Your Thoughts

_____

_____

_____

_____

_____

_____

_____

_____

_____

_____

_____

Subject: First Met, Connection, Responsibilities, and Intimacy
Main Points

Decision-making

Aggressively persuading, forcing your spouse to agree with you, or debating until your spouse is too tired to continue are not effective long-term strategies for conflict resolution or building a mutually satisfying marriage.

Respect each other's gifting and ways of knowing such as by logic, intuition, discernment, etc.

In your quest to get your way it is easy to lose your way.

Give each other grace and mercy.

Focus on what is going right, not only on what is going wrong.

Acceptance and competence

Learn how to receive a compliment without adding your own, "But it could have been…"

Areas of responsibility

Ask what your spouse needs. Do not assume.

Only, never, and always

Once again, do not be distracted by the words *only*, *never*, and *always* during an argument.

Physical intimacy

Be a patient and generous lover.

Acceptance and personal value

Think about your thoughts and feelings. Do not just go through the motions of life.

Experiencing a godly marriage

The experience of a mutually satisfying marriage is limited by the spouse with the least desire and willingness to work towards that goal.

A woman can only experience her fullness as a godly wife to the extent that her husband is willing to be a godly husband.

A man can only experience his fullness as a godly husband to the extent that his wife is willing to be a godly wife.

The least willing-to-be-godly-spouse limits the marriage experience of the other.

Be the spouse who God intended you to be.

Me Questions

1. Are you able to receive a compliment without adding your own, "But it could have been..."? If not, why?

    _____

    _____

    _____

2. What do you think about the statement, "Ask what your spouse needs and do not assume"?

    _____

    _____

    _____

    _____

3. What kind of spouse do you think God intends you to be?

    _____

    _____

    _____

    _____

4. In what ways are you the kind of godly spouse that enables your spouse to enter into the fullness of marriage that God intended for him or her? In what areas could you improve? How would you go about doing that? (Hint: It begins with Romans 12:1-2)

    _____

    _____

    _____

    _____

    _____

    _____

We Questions

5. When you argue, does one of you aggressively persuade and try to force your spouse into agreement until he or she becomes fatigued? If so, does this help the two of you build a mutually satisfying marriage? What is a better way to arrive at a consensus?

    _____

    _____

    _____

6. What do the two of you think is going well in your marriage?

    _____

    _____

    _____

7. How are the two of you unique from each other in the gifts God has given you and in your way of knowing such as by logic, intuition, discernment, etc.?

    _____

    _____

    _____

8. How would each of you describe a patient and generous lover?

    _____

    _____

9. Since the experience of marriage is limited by the person with the least desire and willingness to work, is one of you considerably less willing to work towards building a mutually satisfying marriage than the other? If so, why? What do you gain or lose?

    _____

    _____

    _____

Your Thoughts

_____

_____

_____

_____

_____

_____

_____

_____

_____

_____

_____

_____

_____

_____

_____

_____

_____

_____

_____

Subject: Re: First Met, Connection, Responsibilities, and Intimacy
Main Points

Discernment

Discernment is not logic.

People who treat their spouse with respect usually treat their business partners with the same.

Having a logical mind is a wonderful thing, but some very important forces cannot be analyzed using logic.

Grace and mercy

Give each other grace and mercy.

Grace is giving someone something good they do not deserve, and mercy is withholding something bad that they do deserve.

Imago

The Imago is much more complex than anyone can fully comprehend.

Look for patterns, tendencies, and subtle similarities among your past and current relationships.

Your personality and desires are often developed around the impression that significant others left on you when you were young.

Your personality and desires can develop *counter* to the impressions that others left on you.

Alcoholics often have standards that are difficult to live up to such as, read my mind, anticipate and provide for what I want when I want it, and stay out of my way.

Alcoholics, like people who claim to be perfectionists, can be unpredictable as to what sets them off. And, once you think you understand their rules, they change them.

Defenses and survival strategies

Try not to think harshly of others until you know their desires, needs, fears, wounds, defenses, and assumptions. Given all of those, they may be doing life as well as they can.

When you trigger your spouse's defenses that protect emotional wounds from an earlier period of life, he or she will likely react as though you were the childhood offender. That is why many arguments in retrospect seem childish.

Parents pass on what they have

The vast majority of parents use whatever mental and emotional resources they have to do the best they can for their children.

Parents often pass on to their children the rules and behaviors that helped them either thrive or survive childhood and adulthood.

It is very difficult for parents to give their children what they as children never had or saw in others.

If you want to break the cycle of a destructive family system, you must look to new role models with healthy rules and behaviors.

Power struggle and conscious marriage

The experience of marriage is a shifting and ongoing blend of the power struggle and conscious marriage. It is the amount of time you and your spouse are in one or the other that is a measure of growth and satisfaction in your marriage.

The conscious marriage approach to cooperation gets spouses more of what they want without hurting each other and their marriage relationship in the process.

The power struggle may get you what you want, but it always diminishes your spouse, which over time takes a toll on your relationship.

Abusers do not care who they hurt, or how they diminish their spouse as long as they get what they want when they want it.

The emotional state of abusers is often that of a demanding small child. To be honest, demanding small children are usually more reasonable.

Perfectionism

Conflict in marriage can be a replay of countless painful experiences growing up.

Many people think of God and see Him as having the same characteristics as their earthly father. This idea is best expressed In the Heart of Man, when William Paul Young, author of The Shack, said "It took me all of fifty years to wipe the face of my father completely off the face of God." The opposite is also true. An earthly father who is loving, merciful, and gives grace, lays the foundation for his children to better understand God and His love, mercy, and grace.

There is no perfection in relationships, or anywhere else for that matter.

Self-criticism and identity

People who are intent on criticizing themselves do not stop until they find failure, no matter how small, insignificant, or nonexistent.

Many people who want to be accepted feel strange when they are, and will do their best to beat themselves back to the familiar feeling of not being good enough. They often do this because success is not consistent with their core identity.

Another reason can be they do not want the responsibility of being successful.

Success usually comes in spite of people being harsh with themselves. You should be kind and encouraging to yourself; honestly evaluating when you have succeeded and when you have not.

There is no telling how successful you would be if in addition to your high standards and hard work, you also were kind and encouraging to yourself.

Self-criticism influences how we think God views us. Just as Paul Young had to wipe the face of his father off of God's face, sometimes we need to wipe our own face off of God's face.

Me Questions

1. What experiences have you had with the gift of discernment, either with yourself or with others?

    _____

    _____

    _____

2. When you think about your past and current relationships, what are your patterns and tendencies? Which are mentally, emotionally, spiritually, and physically healthy, and which are not?

    _____

    _____

    _____

3. In what ways have others left their impression on your personality, beliefs, and desires?

    _____

    _____

    _____

    _____

    _____

    _____

4. Have you ever changed your harsh thoughts about someone once you learned more about their desires, needs, fears, wounds, defenses, and assumptions? If so, who, and what was the change?

_____

_____

_____

5. When arguing with your spouse, have you ever noticed yourself falling back to an earlier emotional age? If so, how old, and how did you act?

_____

_____

_____

6. When arguing with your spouse, have you ever noticed him or her falling back to an earlier emotional age? If so, how old, and how did your spouse act?

_____

_____

7. What rules and behaviors did your parents pass on to you that have been helpful?

_____

_____

_____

8. What rules and behaviors did your parents pass on to you that have not been helpful?

_____

_____

_____

_____

9. If it is very difficult for parents to give their children what they as children never had or saw in others, what might be lacking in what you are passing on to your children? What steps are you willing to take in order to meet this need?

_____

_____

_____

10. Who are your role models? What does each role model do that you incorporated into your character?

_____

_____

11. Is it okay for your marriage relationship to not be perfect? If so, how flawed can it be and still be mutually satisfying?

_____

_____

12. What are your non-negotiable requirements for having a mutually satisfying marriage relationship?

_____

_____

_____

13. How harsh is your observing ego? Is it generally a constructive force in your life? If not, when and how can it be harmful?

_____

_____

_____

_____

14. Do you criticize yourself and find failure in everything you do, no matter how small, insignificant, or nonexistent? If so, who taught you how to do that? What benefit do you get from it? If there is no benefit, why would you keep doing it?

_____

_____

_____

15. When you are successful or accepted by others, does it make you feel uncomfortable? If so, do you beat yourself back into the familiar feeling of not being good enough? If so, who taught you that it is wrong to feel good about yourself? How did they teach this?

_____

_____

16. What do you think about the statement, "Success happens in spite of you being harsh with yourself"?

_____

_____

17. What would life be like if you were kind and encouraging to yourself; honestly evaluating when you have succeeded and when you have not?

_____

_____

We Questions

18. What percentage of the time are the two of you in the power struggle phase of your marriage as opposed to a conscious marriage? How can you do better?

_____

_____

_____

19. How do the two of you consciously cooperate to get more of what you both want without hurting each other and your marriage relationship?

_____

_____

_____

_____

20. How has time spent in the power struggle taken a toll on your relationship? How has time invested in a conscious marriage helped your relationship?

_____

_____

_____

_____

21. Is either of you an abuser in that you do not care how much you diminish your spouse as long as you get what you want when you want it? If so, why?

_____

_____

_____

22. Which conflicts in your marriage are replays of painful experiences that either of you had in childhood? When it comes to these conflicts, in what ways are your current emotional reactions similar to those you had during childhood?

_____

_____

_____

_____

_____

_____

Your Thoughts

_____

_____

_____

_____

_____

_____

_____

_____

_____

_____

_____

_____

_____

Subject: Intent, Inner-Child, Wounds, and Defenses
Main Points

Intent

Good intent is important, but does not justify everything a parent does.

You know you were treated poorly as a child if you would not allow someone to treat your child in the same way.

Inner-child

You have multiple facets to your personality that are expressed in different situations such as at work, home, church, etc. Some facets can be more playful and less guarded than others.

Emotional triggers

You can have an emotional game face that you fall back to when you are challenged.

Anger that is not resolved gets stored.

It is in recognizing your triggers and exploring their emotional forces that your wounds are discovered and healing can occur.

You know you hit a trigger when your emotional response is far greater than what the offense warranted.

Triggers can become more sensitive due to daily pressures, recent events, long-term stresses, past wounds, or a combination of the four and others.

When arguing with your spouse, or anyone else for that matter, ask yourself, "How old do I feel emotionally? When did I feel this way before? What is the youngest age I remember feeling this way?

Anger that is stored can be expressed as self-loathing and depression. It can also be expressed throughout the body by an almost unlimited number of symptoms. That is why accepting and processing your anger is so important for your mental, emotional, spiritual, and physical health.

Wounds and defenses

Identifying your wounds, understanding their cause, and removing your defenses around them is a critical part of your healing and growth.

Replacing your automatic reactive and relationship-destructive defenses with intentional and healthy behaviors is an essential part of growth.

Some of your defenses should not be permanently discarded because there may be situations where they are appropriate.

Your defenses are fine if they do not get in the way of God's will for you and something you want more, such as connection with your spouse, children, and friends.

Connection and friends

Your spouse can only be your spouse, and your friends can only be your friends; they are not interchangeable. And, ideally, your spouse should be closer and more trustworthy than any of your friends.

Me Questions

1. What do you think about the statement, "Good intent is important, but does not justify everything a parent does"?

    _____

    _____

2. What do you think about the statement, "You know you were treated poorly as a child if you would not allow someone to treat your child in the same way"? In what ways were you treated that you would not allow for your child?

    _____

    _____

3. What facets do you have to your personality that are expressed in different situations such as at work, home, church, etc.? Are any of these facets emotionally younger than the others?

    _____

    _____

4. Do you believe that unresolved anger gets stored? What anger have you stored?

    _____

    _____

    _____

5. Do you believe that unresolved anger can lead to depression? With whom have you seen that occur and what was the anger? What would you recommend to help them?

_____

_____

_____

6. What triggers do you have and to what wounds are they linked?

_____

_____

_____

7. What do you think about the statement, "It is in recognizing your triggers and exploring their emotional forces that your wounds are discovered and healing can occur"?

_____

_____

8. What type of offense gets a far greater emotional response from you than what is warranted? To what wound is it linked? What other responses might you choose?

_____

_____

_____

9. How susceptible are you to the buildup of daily pressures and long-term stresses? What is the impact of recent events and past wounds on this buildup? What can you do to recognize and ease your pressures and long-term stresses?

_____

_____

_____

10. Think of a recent argument with your spouse and ask yourself, "How old did I feel emotionally? When did I feel that way before? What is the youngest age I remember feeling that way?" Also, how old emotionally did your spouse act during the argument. This will give you insight into why you and your spouse acted the way you did during the argument.

_____

_____

_____

_____

11. If identifying your wounds, understanding their cause, and removing your defenses around them is an essential part of healing and growth, what are your primary wounds and their causes, and what defenses have you built to protect yourself from being re-wounded?

_____

_____

_____

12. How can you replace your reactive and relationship-destructive defenses with intentional and healthy behaviors?

_____

_____

_____

13. Which of your defenses should not be permanently discarded because there may be situations in the future where they are appropriate?

_____

_____

_____

_____

14. Which of your defenses interfere with connecting mentally and emotionally with your spouse, children, friends, and family of origin? How does that interference occur?

_____

_____

We Questions

15. What do the two of you think about the statement, "Your spouse ideally should be closer and more trustworthy than your best friend"? If that is not the case, do you want that to change, or are you content with the way things are?

_____

_____

_____

_____

16. How will the two of you agree to handle each other's triggers when they are activated?

_____

_____

_____

Your Thoughts

_____

_____

_____

_____

_____

_____

_____

_____

_____

Subject: Re: Re: First Met, Connection, Responsibilities, and Intimacy
Main Points

Discernment

Discernment does not always come with 100% certainty.

You can still love people with God's love even if you do not trust them.

Wounds and defenses

Wounds and defenses can be replicated in each generation.

Defensive reactions created for survival in childhood are often used inappropriately in adulthood.

Change is important to prevent issues from your past from getting passed on to your children.

In a conscious marriage, spouses have power *with* each other, not *over* each other.

Perfectionism

Perfection is impossible, so no one can be a perfectionist.

Someone who is labeled a "perfectionist" is in reality a specifist!

Intent

Good intent by others can still leave wounds that need to be addressed and healed.

Stored emotions

Wounds and their stored emotions rarely get better with time.

Talking through an argument

You can process old arguments using new insight.

How old did I feel emotionally?

When did I feel that way before?

What is the youngest age I remember feeling that way?

Many spouses struggle with the same issues, such as feelings of incompetence or self-doubt. The expression of these issues can vary significantly between them.

People often have no trouble recognizing and defending someone else in areas where they have been wounded, but do not do the same for themselves.

When conflicts occur and emotions clash between spouses, it does not mean that either is wrong. One, both, or neither could be wrong.

Connection and friends

A best friend should not be a substitute for your spouse.

Specifist and an irrational perfectionist

You can be a specifist AND an irrational perfectionist by wanting others to do things the specific way you want them done, and expecting perfection from yourself.

Me Questions

1. What do you think about the statement, "You can still love people with God's love even if you do not trust them"?

   _____

   _____

2. As you look back over your family history, what wounds and defenses can you see that were replicated in each generation?

   _____

   _____

   _____

3. What are you doing to prevent issues of your past from getting passed on to your children?

   _____

   _____

   _____

4. What childhood defenses have you used inappropriately in adulthood?

   _____

   _____

   _____

5. What do you think about the statement, "In a conscious marriage, spouses have power *with* each other, not *over* each other"?

    _____

    _____

6. What do you think about the statement, "Perfection is impossible, so no one can be a perfectionist"?

    _____

    _____

7. Do you agree that someone who is labeled a "perfectionist," is in reality a specifist? How have specifists impacted your life?

    _____

    _____

8. Are you a specifist? If so, how do you think this impacts others? Is that impact largely positive or negative?

    _____

    _____

9. Do you have wounds from the good intentions of others that need healing? If so, what are they and how do you think your healing can occur?

    _____

    _____

10. Do you have stored anger from previous wounds? If so, when do you plan on processing this anger? Can your spouse help? If so, how? If not, who can?

    _____

    _____

11. Have you ever defended someone else in an area where you have been wounded, but were unwilling to defend yourself in the same way? If so, what happened?

_____

_____

12. Are you a specifist AND an irrational perfectionist by wanting others to do things the specific way you want them done, and expecting perfection from yourself? If so, do you want to break this pattern? What would happen if you broke it? With what would you replace it? In what ways would grace and mercy be helpful?

_____

_____

We Questions

13. Together, process an old argument using new insights to identify any desires, needs, fears, wounds, defenses, and assumptions that were involved.

_____

_____

14. Do the two of you share any of the same desires, needs, fears, wounds, defenses, and assumptions that you express differently? If so, what are those differences?

_____

_____

_____

15. When conflicts occur and emotions clash between the two of you, is it possible that neither of you is wrong? How can you determine if that is the case?

_____

_____

_____

16. Is either or both of you using a best friend as a substitute for your spouse? If so, how can you grow closer to each other while maintaining your relationship with your friend?

_____

_____

_____

_____

Your Thoughts

_____

_____

_____

_____

_____

_____

_____

_____

_____

_____

_____

_____

_____

_____

_____

_____

_____

_____

_____

Subject: Discernment, Active Listening, and Breaking Old Patterns
Main Points

Discernment

When it comes to your spiritual gifts, step out in faith and trust God to do the rest.

If someone vehemently disagrees with what you are telling them, it may be accurate and something that God has already been speaking to them about, but they have been unwilling to listen to Him.

When you use your spiritual gifts, there is always the possibility you could be wrong. You are not a perfect follower of Jesus and it takes time and practice for you to become competent in your gifting.

Breaking the cycle of triggers and defenses

When it comes to your childhood wounds, quickly recognize and respond differently to familiar patterns.

Your initial recognition of a familiar pattern may first occur days after an encounter. Eventually the lag time shortens until you either recognize the pattern in the moment, or avoid it all together.

Speaking-listening-mirroring-clarifying

When you and your spouse catch yourselves in an old unfruitful pattern, such as the power struggle, either or both of you need to call "Timeout" and take a break to cool off.

Once the two of you get back together, you agree that someone will be the speaker and the other will listen.

The speaker shares small segments of his or her position, and the listener mirrors back by repeating what was heard. Then the listener asks, "Did I repeat that back correctly? The speaker verifies that the mirroring was correct, and if not, provides clarification. After that the listener asks, "Is there more to that?" This cycle is repeated until the person who is speaking believes that the listener understands his or her position.

For mirroring to be effective, it is absolutely essential that the listener is genuinely curious about the speaker's position, and then validates that person's thoughts and feelings.

There is always the temptation for the listener to interrupt in order to defend his or her position. This will only restart the power struggle.

Validating someone's thoughts and feelings does not mean you agree with them. It only means that you understand how and why they think and feel what they do.

People often do not fully understand what they think and feel until they hear themselves speak it out.

The listener's time to speak comes when the speaker believes that the listener understands what he or she is trying to communicate. Then the roles are switched and you repeat the process.

Eventually, you will internalize the spirit of this mirroring process and it will become a natural part of your thinking and dialogue. This means you won't always have to adhere to the rigid structure. Even so, you may need to come back to it if passions are high and listening is low.

Wrestling and renewing your mind

Bring every thought captive to Christ.

> We demolish arguments and every pretension that sets itself up against the knowledge of God, and we take captive every thought to make it obedient to Christ. (Corinthians 10:5)

Offer yourself as a living sacrifice.

> Therefore, I urge you, brothers and sisters, in view of God's mercy, to offer your bodies as a living sacrifice, holy and pleasing to God—this is your true and proper worship. 2 Do not conform to the pattern of this world, but be transformed by the renewing of your mind. Then you will be able to test and approve what God's will is—his good, pleasing and perfect will. (Romans 12: 1-2)

When thinking about your spouse, think on positive traits.

> "Finally, brothers and sisters, whatever is true, whatever is noble, whatever is right, whatever is pure, whatever is lovely, whatever is admirable—if anything is excellent or praiseworthy—think about such things." (Philippians 4:8)

Engaging with each other becomes easier when both of you establish new rules and behaviors for interacting, and you experience the joy of safe and effective communication.

Unfortunately, what often happens is that couples revert back to their childhood emotions and lash out at each other to defend themselves, prevent the re-wounding of old wounds, or to simply get what they want. The opposite usually occurs in that old wounds are re-wounded, new wounds are added, what is wanted is rarely received, and the use of unproductive defenses are reinforced.

If lashing out and fighting back is the norm for you and your spouse, it can eventually result in the death of your relationship and possibly divorce.

God can bring all relationships back from the dead if both people are willing to do the work, and have the tools, insight, and energy to do so.

Wanting a great marriage is essential, but not sufficient. You and your spouse must do the hard work needed to build one; especially when you don't want to.

Awareness and stopping the cycle

Awareness of the rules, behaviors, and assumptions that were passed down to you through the generations is the first step in stopping the dysfunction in a family, or at the least, in slowing it down considerably.

Sometimes the most important and meaningful act that parents can do is to work through their painful past in order to build a better future for themselves, their spouse, and their children.

It is the painful parts of your past that can drive your negative thoughts and emotions, which can strongly determine how you relate to your family and others.

Practice learning about your triggers using an argument from the past. That way you don't have to deal with the content and the emotions in real time.

A godly pattern of resolution is when 1) your reaction to your spouse is triggered based on a past wound, 2) you and your spouse talk about the trigger and link it to your past, 3) you surface the past wound and are intentional about its healing, and 4) you take steps to avoid the trigger in the future. The result is healing and growth for the past and the present, and preventing a reoccurrence in the future.

Me Questions

1. When it comes to your spiritual gifts, are you able to step out in faith and trust God to do the rest? If not, what could help build your confidence and trust?

    _____

    _____

    _____

2. Are you someone who does not fully understand what you think and feel until you hear yourself speak it out? This is often referred to as being an auditory processor. How can your spouse help you when you are trying to process your thoughts and feelings? How can you help your spouse help you?

    _____

    _____

    _____

3. Is it possible to bring every thought captive to Christ? If not, why would the Apostle
    Paul write something like that?

    _____

    _____

4. What does "…offer your bodies as a living sacrifice…" mean to you?

    _____

    _____

5. What would happen if you focused your thoughts on one or two of your spouse's
    positive attributes?

    "Finally, brothers and sisters, whatever is true, whatever is noble, whatever is
    right, whatever is pure, whatever is lovely, whatever is admirable—if anything
    is excellent or praiseworthy—think about such things." (Philippians 4:8)

    _____

    _____

    _____

6. What would happen if you focused on one or two of your own positive attributes?

    _____

    _____

    _____

7. What do you think about the statement, "Sometimes the most important and meaningful
    act you can do for your children is to work through your own painful past in order to
    build a better future for you, your spouse, and your children."?

    _____

    _____

    _____

    _____

8. What painful parts of your past drive negative thoughts and emotions that currently influence how you relate to your family and others? What are those thoughts and emotions? What patterns of behavior are involved?

_____

_____

_____

We Questions

9. What would happen if when the two of you are in a familiar unfruitful pattern, one of you called "Timeout" and the two of you took a break to cool off? Would you be able to come back together and continue in a more effective way? If not, why?

_____

_____

10. What do the two of you think about the idea that "Validating someone's thoughts and feelings does not mean you agree with them. It only means that you understand how and why they think and feel what they do."? Are you able to do this? If not, why?

_____

_____

11. What new rules and behaviors for interacting with each other would you like to establish in order to experience the joy of safe and productive communication?

_____

_____

12. If the two of you often revert back to your childhood emotions and defend yourselves by lashing out at each other in an effort to prevent the re-wounding of your old wounds, how will you break this pattern? Do you enjoy the pattern?

_____

_____

13. Do the two of you believe the statement, "God can bring all relationships back from the dead if both people are willing to do the work, and have the tools, insight, and energy to do so"?

_____

_____

_____

14) What thoughts do the two of you have about the statement, "Wanting a great marriage is essential, but not sufficient. You and your spouse must do the hard work needed to build one; especially when you don't want to"?

_____

_____

_____

_____

15) What rules, behaviors, and assumptions about marriage were passed down to the two of you from your respective families of origin that you must either stop, or at the least, slow down considerably?

_____

_____

16) What do the two of you think about the following?

A godly pattern of resolution is when 1) your reaction to your spouse is triggered based on a past wound, 2) you and your spouse talk about the trigger and link it to your past, 3) you surface the past wound and are intentional about its healing, and 4) you take steps to avoid the trigger in the future. The result is healing and growth for the past and the present, and preventing a reoccurrence in the future.

_____

_____

_____

_____

Your Thoughts

_____

_____

_____

_____

_____

_____

_____

_____

_____

_____

_____

_____

_____

_____

_____

_____

_____

_____

_____

_____

_____

Subject: Betrayal
Main Points

Improvement begins by failing for shorter and shorter periods of time.

No one can take captive every thought to make it obedient to Christ.

Me Question

1. What do you think about the statement, "Improvement begins by failing for shorter and shorter periods of time"?

_____

_____

We Question

2. How can you help each other fail for shorter and shorter periods of time?

_____

_____

Your Thoughts

_____

_____

_____

_____

_____

_____

_____

_____

_____

_____

Subject: Re: Betrayal
Main Points

Betrayal and sincerity

Weigh carefully in your mind and spirit not only what you share with someone, but also what you are offered by others.

Be careful about what you receive into your thinking from others.

If you are uncomfortable with what someone tells you, it is perfectly fine to say, "I do not receive that."

Sincerity is not enough because everyone has been sincerely wrong at one time or another.

Betrayal is when people intentionally take advantage of your relationship to achieve their own gains, or have a total disregard for your relationship when pursuing their own agenda.

Friends are the ones who stab you in the back because they are the ones you let back there. This doesn't mean you should not trust your friends, or your spouse, it just means you need to trust Jesus for your healing if things go poorly.

All relationships have risks and Matthew 10:16 is still relevant today. Jesus told His disciples, "I am sending you out like sheep among wolves. Therefore be as shrewd as snakes and as innocent as doves." Don't be surprised to find wolves faithfully attending church.

Manipulation or motivation

Manipulation is getting someone to achieve *your goal*, of which, that person is unaware.

Motivation is helping someone achieve *their goal*, of which, they are aware and have asked you to help.

There are couples where one or both spouses only want the appearance of working on their relationship and have no intention of changing anything except their spouse's behavior.

Do not impose your marriage goals and roles on others. They must build their own unique mutually satisfying marriage.

Impossible-to-perform verses

Impossible-to-perform verses are not high bars for you to achieve, rather, they are the Holy Spirit's power for you to receive.

All verses in Scripture are beyond your natural ability to fulfill and you need God working in you to will and to act in a way that fulfills His good purpose.

> Therefore, my dear friends, as you have always obeyed—not only in my presence, but now much more in my absence—continue to work out your salvation with fear and trembling, [13] for it is God who works in you to will and to act in order to fulfill his good purpose. (Philippians 2:12-13)

You work out your salvation with God who works in you to will and to act. Remember that Jesus fulfilled the Law as Paul writes in Romans Chapter 8.

> Therefore, there is now no condemnation for those who are in Christ Jesus, [2] because through Christ Jesus the law of the Spirit who gives life has set you free from the law of sin and death. [3] For what the law was powerless to do because it was weakened by the flesh, God did by sending his own Son in the likeness of sinful flesh to be a sin offering. And so he condemned sin in the flesh, [4] in order that the righteous requirement of the law might be fully met in us, who do not live according to the flesh but according to the Spirit. (Romans 8:1-4)

To stay in the Spirit, you need a continual renewing of your mind.

> Therefore, I urge you, brothers and sisters, in view of God's mercy, to offer your bodies as a living sacrifice, holy and pleasing to God—this is your true and proper worship. [2] Do not conform to the pattern of this world, but be transformed by the renewing of your mind. Then you will be able to test and approve what God's will is—his good, pleasing and perfect will. (Romans 12:1-2)

You cannot do any of this Christian stuff on your own.

Sometimes you can *act* like Jesus, but Jesus wants to *live* in you, and *work* through you; not have you *acting* like Him in your flesh.

You are the temple of the Holy Spirit.

> Do you not know that your bodies are temples of the Holy Spirit, who is in you, whom you have received from God? You are not your own; [20] you were bought at a price. Therefore honor God with your bodies. (1 Corinthians 6:19-20)

Anything spiritual you do begins with you offering yourself as a living sacrifice and realizing that you are the temple of the Holy Spirit. Then God can produce His will in you, and do His purposes through you.

Going through the motions

Going through the motions in your marriage is not bad if it is godly obedience that overcomes temporary feelings of disconnection.

Unfortunately, going through the motions can also serve the purpose of ungodly avoidance that solidifies permanent feelings of disconnection.

Godly obedience maintains your relationship, while ungodly avoidance starves it.

Godly obedience is about function and substance, while ungodly avoidance is about function and appearance.

Godly obedience supports your healing and growth, while ungodly avoidance maintains wounds and defenses.

As for a relationship being dead or not, if spouses are asking the question, it isn't.

Some have said that the opposite of love is indifference.

Unrecognized success

Disagreements are not a sign of failure.

When you find yourself in an argument with your spouse, you have not failed. Arguments happen. Success is in how quickly you reach an understanding by talking and listening to each other.

Garden of Eden mutual love

According to the Pre-Fall model of marriage, you and your spouse should have mutual love for each other.

You and your spouse are to love each other as Christ loves the Church, and in the same way as you love yourselves.

It is difficult to argue that you and your spouse should not be growing in your ability to have the same love for each other because both of you are being conformed to the image of Jesus.

Of course, this is the ideal, and the reality is that there will always be a difference between you and your spouse in the ability and choice to love each other.

We cannot surprise God

God appreciates your honesty with Him.

You cannot surprise God with anything.

When God accepts you, He already knows everything you have done and everything you will ever think, say, and do; your successes and your failures. On what basis in the future would He ever reject you? The only one surprised in the future by what you think, say, and do is you.

Me Questions

1. How do you weigh in your mind and spirit what people offer you in terms of insight or advice?

   _____

   _____

2. How have people intentionally taken advantage of your relationship with them to achieve their own gains? Were there any warning signs? If so, what were they?

   _____

   _____

3. What do you think about the statement, "Friends are the ones who stab you in the back because they are the ones you let back there"?

   _____

   _____

4. What are the risks in relationships?

   _____

   _____

5. Define manipulation.

   _____

   _____

6. Define motivation.

   _____

   _____

7. Why would a spouse only want the appearance of working on his or her marriage relationship and have no intention of changing anything except their spouse's behavior?

    _____

    _____

    _____

8. What do you think about the statement, "Do not impose your marriage goals and roles on others. They must build their own unique mutually satisfying marriage"?

    _____

    _____

9. Why would the Bible include "impossible-to-perform" verses?

    _____

    _____

10. What can you do in your own strength?

    _____

    _____

11. When and how do you offer yourself and your marriage to God as a living sacrifice?

    _____

    _____

12. What are your struggles with self-condemnation? (See Romans 8:1-4)

    _____

    _____

    _____

13. What are your struggles with condemnation from others? (See Romans 8:1-4)

_____

_____

_____

14. What is the difference between you *acting* like Jesus, or letting Him *work* in and through you?

_____

_____

15. What does it mean for you to be the temple of the Holy Spirit?

_____

_____

16. What do you think about the following? Anything spiritual you do begins with offering yourself as a living sacrifice and realizing you are the temple of the Holy Spirit. Then God can produce His will in you, and do His purposes through you.

_____

_____

17. What is the difference between godly obedience and ungodly avoidance when it comes to "going through the motions" in a marriage?

_____

_____

18. Why is avoidance such a commonly used strategy when there are problems in a marriage relationship?

_____

_____

19. What are the characteristics of a dead relationship?

_____

_____

20. Is it true that the opposite of love is indifference? Can you be angry and indifferent? What reasons support your thinking on this?

_____

_____

21. Why would it matter for you to be honest with God? He knows everything anyhow.

_____

_____

22. What are the implications of the following?

When God accepts you, He already knows everything you have done and everything you will ever think, say, and do; your successes and your failures. On what basis in the future would He ever reject you? The only one surprised by what you eventually think, say, and do in the future is you.

_____

_____

_____

We Questions

23. What can you do as a couple to prevent disagreements from becoming arguments?

_____

_____

_____

_____

24. When you have disagreements with each other, how long does it usually take to reach an understanding? The longer it takes means the more likely it is that you are dealing with childhood wounds and defenses.

_____

_____

_____

25. Does it make sense that according to a Pre-Fall model of marriage a husband is to love his wife as Christ loves the Church, and his wife is also to love him as Christ loves the church? Does it make sense that a husband is to love his wife as he loves himself, and his wife is also to love him as she loves herself? What argument can you make that a wife should have less love for her husband than he has for her, or a husband should have less love for his wife than she has for him?

_____

_____

_____

_____

_____

Your Thoughts

_____

_____

_____

_____

_____

_____

_____

_____

Subject: No Mentors to Follow
Main Points

What you imitate from others needs to be the result of the same Holy Spirit in you who was in the Lord, and who was in Paul, and who raised Jesus from the dead.

You cannot produce from your flesh what can only be produced with the Holy Spirit.

Everyone separately and as a couple struggles with the pattern of Romans 7:15 that says, "I do not understand what I do. For what I want to do I do not do, but what I hate I do"?

You need practical and doable actions for living out the renewing of your mind.

Me Question

1. Is your marriage often patterned after Romans 7:15, 'I do not understand what I do. For what I want to do I do not do, but what I hate I do'? If so, why? How can you do better at changing unfruitful patterns? (hint: By offering something that is living.)

    _____

    _____

We Questions

2. Who do each of you look to as mentors for your marriage? How is the Holy Spirit active in the lives of your mentors?

    _____

    _____

3. What practical and doable actions do each of you want the other to do as an expression of love for you?

    _____

    _____

    _____

    _____

Your Thoughts

_____
_____
_____
_____
_____
_____
_____
_____
_____
_____
_____
_____
_____
_____
_____

Subject: Re: No Mentors to Follow
Main Points

Stay on God's altar

You do not have to get down off of God's altar to get on with your day. Your day can come to you as you maintain your position on His altar.

Storms and waves of life can rage against you and wash you off of God's altar. And when that happens you have to get back on.

The storms are often what causes people to return to the altar from which they wandered away during good weather.

Strengths and weaknesses (Bob and Beth in the novel)

Spouses often struggle with the same issues, such as feeling inadequate, but their individual expression of their struggle is unique.

It is important for you and your spouse to accept each other's strengths and appreciate how each of you is a unique expression of Jesus.

You can study your spouse's strengths and use him or her as a role model to develop your own.

Your challenge is to grow in your spouse's strengths; not resent them.

Sometimes a weakness can be addressed by redirecting an existing strength in the appropriate way.

It is fine for you to have individual preferences and they can be good for your marriage relationship.

You need to accept who you are and how you were created.

Psalm 139:14, "I praise you because I am fearfully and wonderfully made; your works are wonderful, I know that full well."

You would do well not to value yourself according to only the world's values and expectations.

In a healthy marriage each spouse recognizes the contributions the other makes to his or her successes.

Connecting

Do not let the urgent matters of life dictate and crowd out what is important.

The defense of pouting and withdrawing is rarely helpful and is a characteristic of the power struggle.

Communicating is a characteristic of a conscious marriage.

Your spouse is often well-suited to wound you in the same way you were by your parents and caregivers. The challenge is for you and your spouse to heal and grow out of any destructive patterns.

Be intentional in making time for your spouse.

Have a regular date night.

When you are out to dinner with your spouse, be with your spouse and do not let yourself be distracted. No checking your cell phone. No looking around the restaurant for people you know. No wandering off in your head to plan what you will be working on later that night or the next day.

When you are on a date with your spouse, you belong to each other. Period.

When you are mad at your spouse, it is your responsibility to let him or her know.

If you are in a bad mood or mad about something that has nothing to do with your spouse, it is helpful to let him or her know so he or she will not assume the worst.

Some spouses assume they have done nothing wrong unless their spouse explicitly tells them what they are upset about.

Your patterned behaviors towards others are learned responses.

There's a reason for everything you do; even if it makes no sense to anyone else, or even to you.

When a patterned behavior gets in the way of something you want more, it is time to break the pattern, and establish a new and more effective behavior.

Role models are all around us

There are role models all around you.

Almost anyone can be a role model of something, no matter how small, that you can build into your character to improve yourself and/or your marriage.

Do not let your own insecurities, poor self-esteem, or harsh judgments blind you to your spouse's strengths and image of Jesus.

You can learn from anyone; even if it is what not to do.

Me Questions

1. What are your thoughts on the following statement? You do not have to get down off of God's altar to get on with your day. Your day can come to you as you maintain your position on His altar.

    _____

    _____

2. Do the storms of life wash you off of God's altar, chase you back onto it, or both? How do you get back on?

_____

_____

3. Why can it be difficult for spouses to accept each other's strengths, and appreciate each other's unique expression of Jesus?

_____

_____

4. In which strengths can your spouse serve as a role model for you?

_____

_____

5. What can blind you or others to your spouse's strengths?

_____

_____

_____

_____

_____

_____

6. Is it a challenge for you to grow in your spouse's strengths and not resent them? If so, why?

_____

_____

_____

_____

7. Which of your existing strengths could be successfully redirected to another area of your life?

_____

_____

8. Is it difficult for you to accept who you are and how you were created? If so, what do others see as your strengths that you might not be appreciating?

_____

_____

_____

9. What do you think about the statement, "You would do well not to value yourself according to only the world's values and expectations"? What standards do you use to value yourself? What are your expectations of you? Are they reasonable? If not, why?

_____

_____

_____

10. How often do the urgent matters of life dictate and crowd out what is important to you? What are the urgent matters in your life and what can you do to change their impact?

_____

_____

_____

11. What do you think about the following? Your patterned behaviors towards others are a learned response. There is a reason for everything you do; even if it makes no sense to anyone else, or even you.

_____

_____

12. How can you break patterns of ineffective behaviors and give rise to new ones?

_____

_____

13. What do you think about the statement, "Almost anyone can be a role model to you for something, no matter how small"?

_____

_____

14. Who has taught you what not to do in your marriage? What did you observe? What will you do differently?

_____

_____

_____

15. What do you think about the following? You can learn from others in the context of their faith how they express love, joy, peace, forbearance, kindness, goodness, faithfulness, gentleness, and self-control. Then you can cultivate and express your own.

_____

_____

_____

We Questions

16. Is it fine and beneficial to your marriage relationship for the two of you to have individual preferences? Which preferences do the two of you have that differ from each other?

_____

_____

_____

17. In what ways have the two of you contributed to each other's success?

18. Is the defense of pouting and withdrawing used often by one or both of you? If so, does it work better than communicating? Recall that pouting and withdrawing are characteristic of the power struggle, and communicating is characteristic of a conscious marriage.

19. Is it true that each of you is well-suited to wound the other in the same way as in childhood by parents and caregivers? If so, how? The challenge is to grow out of any wounding patterns.

20. What are your thoughts on the following? Be intentional in making time for your spouse. Have a regular date night. When you are out to dinner with your spouse, be with your spouse and do not let yourself be distracted. No checking your cell phone. No looking around the restaurant for people you know. No wandering off in your head to plan what you will be working on later that night or the next day. When you are on a date, you belong to each other. Period.

21. When one of you is mad at the other, is it the responsibility of the one who is mad to let the other know? If it is, what is the best way to do that. If not, why?

22. When one of you is in a bad mood or mad about something that has nothing to do with the other, do you think it is helpful to let him or her know so he or she will not assume the worst? If not, why?

_____

_____

23. Would it be okay if both of you assumed you have done nothing wrong unless your spouse explicitly tells you exactly what he or she is upset about? If not, why?

_____

_____

Your Thoughts

_____

_____

_____

_____

_____

_____

_____

_____

_____

_____

_____

_____

_____

_____

_____

_____

Subject: Our Spouse as a Role Model and Changing Patterns
Main Points

People often do to others what was done to them.

Since it is God who creates everyone along with their unique set of character traits, it isn't fair for you to judge others on how God did not create them.

People often judge others harshly who are similar to them.

Emotional pain does not respond solely to intellectual explanations.

Sometimes your spouse and children want your affirmation, not your opinion.

If you want to help someone with a decision, ask meaningful questions.

You and your spouse will improve your marriage skills together as you communicate more openly and honestly; speaking the truth in love.

It is important to be able to trust each other with your creativity.

Assist each other's creativity and reflect back the wisdom God has given you.

Before going on a date with your spouse, it can be helpful to decide what time the date will end.

Be alert for actions and attitudes that stem from your own insecurities such as fear of abandonment.

Intensity does not always mean anger.

Learn your spouse's moods and patterns.

Criticizing your spouse when you are frustrated about other things is a common pattern that is not effective.

Once you recognize a pattern, it is possible for you to change it.

Be intentional and communicate; this is simple, but not easy.

Me Questions

1. Why do people often do to others what was done to them?

_____

_____

_____

_____

_____

2. Why do some people judge others for how God did not create them?

    _____

    _____

    _____

3. Why does emotional pain not respond solely to intellectual explanations? What is a better response?

    _____

    _____

4. Why do people often judge others harshly who are similar to them?

    _____

    _____

5. What do you think about the statement, "Sometimes your spouse and children want your affirmation, not your opinion"?

    _____

    _____

6. Why is asking meaningful questions more helpful than telling people what to do?

    _____

    _____

7. Which of your actions and attitudes stem from your insecurities such as fear of abandonment?

    _____

    _____

8. Is it true that intensity does not always mean anger? What about your intensity? How would you like others to respond to your intensity?

_____

_____

_____

We Questions

9. How can you improve your marriage skills together as you communicate more openly and honestly; speaking the truth in love?

_____

_____

_____

10. Can you trust each other with your creativity? If not, why? How can the two of you become even better at being trustworthy in this area?

_____

_____

11. Why is it important for both of you to learn each other's moods and patterns? What are the moods and patterns in your relationship? What moods and patterns do each of you have with your children and others?

_____

_____

12. Do you criticize each other when you are frustrated about other things? If so, why? How can you change?

_____

_____

13. Do you think that once you recognize a pattern in your marriage, it is possible for the two of you to change it by being intentional and communicating? If so, what specific steps would you take?

_____

_____

_____

_____

_____

Your Thoughts

_____

_____

_____

_____

_____

_____

_____

_____

_____

_____

_____

_____

_____

_____

_____

_____

_____

_____

Subject: Self-Judgment and the Strong Emotions of Others
Main Points

Judging ourselves and others

It is easy for people to judge others when they do not have all of the facts.

God is the only One capable of judging accurately because He is the only One with all of the facts and the righteousness to do so.

The most important fact of all is that Jesus died for your sins and the sins of those people whom you do not understand.

There isn't an increment of time small enough in anyone's life that would not declare him or her a sinner and worthy of judgment.

You have enough facts about yourself to repent, but not enough to judge yourself. You have to wait for the Lord to do that.

You should not judge your actions in the past based on the insight you have now. That was then, and the blood of Christ was sufficient for then, and this is now, and the blood of Christ is sufficient for now.

It isn't fair for you to compare your inside thoughts, feelings, and struggles to the outside appearance of others.

Feelings of inadequacy are often the result of self-directed judgment.

Give yourself no more and no less grace than you would give to your best friend.

When safety and nurturing are high, people are freer to bring out their creativity.

Treating emotional pain with intellectual explanations

Someone's emotional pain is rarely treatable solely with intellectual explanations.

You can only *offer* people what you have, and you can only *tell* them about the other things that you have *heard* about.

If you were not taught how to process your emotions when you were growing up, you need to fill in that void by learning to do so later in life.

Once you learn how to experience, tolerate, and process your own emotions, you will be better able to do the same with the emotions of others.

The strong emotions of *others* can make *you* feel uncomfortable.

For some Christians, experiencing the strong emotions of others is very uncomfortable. Their response is often to administer a quick intellectualized slap-a-verse answer that is more designed to soothe the uncomfortable feelings of the one offering the answer than the recipient. This attempt can be little more than, "Gee, your emotional wound and pain is gross and makes me feel bad. Let me slap this bandage verse on it. Now, go and act healed so I will feel better."

Appreciation of each other begins with understanding, and understanding begins with listening.

Your marriage is the only one of its kind in all of human history and all of human future. Make it all that it was meant to be.

Everyone is "odd" in their own way.

It's been said that you should only fight battles big enough to matter and small enough to win. It is good to fight actual sin and be content to leave the "oddness" of others alone.

Marriage is the most intimate form of a relationship between believers.

Be diligently obedient in your healing and growth as you work on your marriage in the power of the Holy Spirit.

Me Questions

1. Why can it be difficult for you to interact with people you don't understand? How can you be more effective at this?

    _____

    _____

    _____

2. What do you think about the statement, "You have enough facts about yourself to repent, but not enough to judge yourself"?

    _____

    _____

3. Do you struggle with self-directed judgment? If so, in what ways and who taught you how to do that?

    _____

    _____

    _____

    _____

4. When you find yourself in a pattern of self-judgment, to whom do you compare yourself?

    _____

    _____

5. When you compare yourself to others, how fair is it for you to compare your inside thoughts, feelings, and struggles to their outside appearance? If it isn't, why?

    _____

    _____

6. What do you think about the statement, "Give yourself no more and no less grace than you would give to your best friend"?

    _____

    _____

7. What do you think about the statement, "Once you learn how to experience, tolerate, and process your own emotions, you will be better able to do the same with the emotions of others"? How well do you handle your strong emotions?

    _____

    _____

8. Do you feel uncomfortable in the presence of the strong emotions of others? If so, why? How were strong emotions handled in your family when you were growing up.

    _____

    _____

9. Do you have a tendency to offer intellectualized slap-a-verse answers to others or yourself? Do those kinds of answers help? What would be more helpful?

    _____

    _____

10. If appreciation of each other begins with understanding, and understanding begins with listening, is it difficult for you to listen to someone you don't understand? If so, why, and how can you do better?

_____

_____

11. What do you think about the statement, "You are odd in your own way, which is what makes you unique, and fearfully and wonderfully made"?

_____

_____

12. What battles in your life are too small to matter and too big to win?

_____

_____

We Questions

13. If one or both of you were not taught how to process your emotions when you were growing up, can you fill that void by learning to do so with each other? How can the two of you help each other in this area?

_____

_____

14. Do you find it incredible that your marriage is the only one of its kind in all of human history and all of human future? What makes your marriage unique? What do you think God's intent is for your marriage?

_____

_____

_____

_____

Your Thoughts

_____

_____

_____

_____

_____

_____

_____

_____

_____

_____

_____

_____

_____

Subject: The Bible's Hidden Book of Marriage
Main Points

Submit to each other out of reverence for Christ

The Bible is a book about relationships: relationships between Christians and their personal relationship with God.

The Bible speaks from a Post-Fall perspective about relationships with strangers, neighbors, family, enemies, friends, employers, Christians, husbands, slaves, children, and wives. Slaves, children, and wives fall under the category of property.

While Paul's writings do not unambiguously support the Pre-Fall perspective of Adam and Eve ruling coequally in the Garden of Eden, he comes as close as he can within the context of his culture.

Three times in Ephesians chapter 5, Paul tells husbands to love their wives.

The first is in verse 25,

> "Husbands, love your wives, just as Christ loved the church and gave himself up for her"

The second is in verse 28,

> "In this same way, husbands ought to love their wives as their own bodies. He who loves his wife loves himself."

And the third is in verse 33,

> "However, each one of you also must love his wife as he loves himself, and the wife must respect her husband."

Yet in the face of these three *love your wife* directives, some men cling singularly to verses 22 and 23,

> "Wives, submit yourselves to your own husbands as you do to the Lord. 23 For the husband is the head of the wife as Christ is the head of the church, his body, of which he is the Savior."

Paul's commanding a man to love his wife at that time was the equivalent of commanding him to love his property such as a dog or blanket.

Being commanded to love your wife would have been especially strange to Paul's male readers since a common Jewish prayer for males in leadership was to thank God they were not born a woman.

In essence, Paul is saying to love and submit to your wife, a woman, whom you own and thank God every day you were not born to be.

There is an excellent sermon called, The Spirit-filled Marriage (I Believe in the

Church, pt. 10) by Josh Miller at Harvest Vineyard Church in Ames, Iowa. It is located at https://www.harvestvc.org/sermonaudiorss.xml. The actual sermon starts at the 9 minute mark.

Specific guidance for a Pre-Fall marriage

The specific guidance in the Bible for couples who believe God's will for marriage was best expressed prior to the Fall is found in the verses that describe how Christians should interact with one another and those around them.

The marriage relationship is an extension of being members of the Body of Christ, which means it not only *encompasses* how two Christians are to relate to each other, it also provides for an exclusive and even greater connection of intimacy when they are spouses. This is referred to as, "Yes, and even more." Yes, Scripture applies to their relationship as individual believers, and even more as spouses.

God wants husbands to treat their wives at least as well and even better than they treat anyone else, and He wants wives to do the same to their husband. This means that the scriptures that apply to believers can be adapted and personalized to your spouse.

There's a big difference between *creatively adapting* Scripture to build and strengthen a marriage, and *deliberately distorting* Scripture to establish and preserve an abuser's dominance.

Personalizing a verse is substituting one noun for another that is more personal. For example:

'"A new command I give you: Love **one another**. As I have loved you, so you must love **one another**."' (John 13:34)

If Jesus was speaking to you directly about your marriage he could just as easily have said,

"A new command I give you: Love **<your spouse's name>**. As I have loved you, so you must love **<your spouse's name>**.

The second example is,

"By this everyone will know that you are my disciples, if you love **one another**." (John 13:35)

Using the singular form of disciples, the personalized version becomes,

"By this everyone will know that you are my disciple, if you love **<your spouse's name>**."

Personalizing verses that can relate to marriage makes it much more difficult to gloss over them as just theoretical or intellectual suggestions. It makes them real in the daily experience of how you and your spouse should relate to each other.

You are to be an intentional giver of love to your spouse, not an entitled consumer of theirs.

Abusive relationships

Each person in an abusive relationship needs to seek God for clear direction on whether to stay or leave in the power of the Holy Spirit.

If God hates divorce, which He does, He hates even more the behaviors that lead to it.

God does not collude with an abuser by holding one spouse down with His Word, while the other torments him or her by continually and intentionally inflicting mental, emotional, spiritual, and/or physical harm.

Applying any Scripture to a hurting marriage relationship begins with Romans 12:1-2

> Therefore, I urge you, brothers and sisters, in view of God's mercy, to offer your bodies as a living sacrifice, holy and pleasing to God—this is your true and proper worship. 2 Do not conform to the pattern of this world, but be transformed by the renewing of your mind. Then you will be able to test and approve what God's will is—his good, pleasing and perfect will.

And, the appropriate application of Scripture to a hurting marriage can only happen within the context of a personal relationship with God as described in Philippians 2:12-13.

> 12 Therefore, my dear friends, as you have always obeyed—not only in my presence, but now much more in my absence—continue to work out your salvation with fear and trembling, 13 for it is God who works in you to will and to act in order to fulfill his good purpose.

Three cautions about personalizing verses to a marriage relationship.

1) Personalizing verses in the appropriate context is offered as guidance for discovering God's original will for your marriage; not for changing the meaning of any verse.

2) Converting verses about how Christians should behave towards one another into specific statements about your marriage relationship must not be used for manipulation.

3) Be discerning when anyone interprets Scripture because abusers, or those who are sincerely wrong, can distort anything to suit their purpose.

Me Questions

1. What do you think about the following?

    The marriage relationship between Christian spouses is an extension of being members of the Body of Christ. This means that specific guidance in the Bible for couples who believe God's will for marriage was best expressed prior to the Fall is found in verses that describe how Christians should interact with one another and those around them. This is referred to as, "Yes, and even more." Yes, Scripture applies to your relationship as individual believers in the Body of Christ, and even more as spouses.

    _____

    _____

    _____

    _____

2. What are your thoughts on the statement, "You are to be an intentional giver of love to your spouse, not an entitled consumer of theirs"?

    _____

    _____

    _____

3. What do you think about the statement, "If God hates divorce, which He does, He hates even more the behaviors that lead to it"?

    _____

    _____

    _____

4. Why would God collude with an abuser by holding one spouse down with His Word, while he or she torments the other by intentionally and continually inflicting mental, emotional, spiritual, and/or physical harm?

    _____

    _____

5. Applying any Scripture to a hurting marriage relationship begins with Romans 12:1-2 in the context of a relationship with God as described in Philippians 2:12-13. Do these two passages describe your approach to your marriage? If so, great! If not, how can you do better?

_____

_____

We Question

6. What verses would the two of you personalize for your marriage relationship?

_____

_____

Your Thoughts

_____

_____

_____

_____

_____

_____

_____

_____

_____

_____

_____

_____

_____

_____

_____

Subject: Re: The Bible's Hidden Book of Marriage
Main Points

Specific guidance for a Pre-Fall marriage

Hidden in the verses regarding how Christians should interact with one another and others is God's will for living out your marriage relationship. This transcends any cultural view of marriage.

God's Pre-Fall will for living out a marriage is revealed in His Redeemed Church.

God redeemed His Church and the implementation of marriage at the same time and in the same way through Jesus.

According to the Pre-Fall model of marriage, everything about marriage between the Fall and Jesus' resurrection was the same detour under the law that people experienced individually.

From a Post-Fall perspective, many wives would rather be their husband's brother in Christ than his wife!

Transitioning of church culture

Two types of transitioning in the Bible are:

1) When individuals are alienated from God, and they accept Jesus as their Savior to become members of the Body of Christ.

2) When the Body of Christ matures and transitions over thousands of years in how it interprets and applies Scripture.

The thought of a maturing Church over thousands of years can be unsettling, but it is good to be beyond the eras of the Crusades, Inquisition, and when Scripture was used by some to justify slavery.

Me Questions

1. What do you think about the statement, "God's Pre-Fall will for living out a marriage is revealed in His Redeemed Church. He redeemed His Church and the implementation of marriage at the same time and in the same way through Jesus"?

_____

_____

_____

_____

_____

2. What do you think about the statement, "According to the Pre-Fall model of marriage, everything about marriage between the Fall and Jesus' resurrection was the same detour under the law that people experienced individually"?

_____

_____

3. Have you transitioned from being alienated from God to becoming a member of the Body of Christ by accepting Jesus as your Savior? If not, what is preventing you from doing so? If you have, how does that influence your marriage relationship?

_____

_____

4. Do you believe there can be a maturing of the Body of Christ over thousands of years in how it interprets and applies Scripture, such as moving beyond the eras of the Crusades, Inquisition, and when Scripture was used by some to justify slavery? What are the dangers around this thought? What are the assumptions around the belief that the Body of Christ cannot mature over time?

_____

_____

_____

_____

We Questions

5. If the two of you advocate a Post-Fall marriage, can you understand why some wives would rather be their husband's brother in Christ? If so, why? If not, why?

_____

_____

_____

_____

_____

_____

6. Would either of you want to be married to someone like you? If not, why?

    _____

    _____

    _____

7. What changes, if any, would either of you make in yourselves to become more like a spouse that you would desire? They all begin with Romans 12:1-2.

    Therefore, I urge you, brothers and sisters, in view of God's mercy, to offer your bodies as a living sacrifice, holy and pleasing to God—this is your true and proper worship. 2 Do not conform to the pattern of this world, but be transformed by the renewing of your mind. Then you will be able to test and approve what God's will is—his good, pleasing and perfect will.

    _____

    _____

Your Thoughts

_____

_____

_____

_____

_____

_____

_____

_____

_____

_____

_____

_____

Subject: Re: Re: The Bible's Hidden Book of Marriage
Main Points

Transitioning and maturing of Church culture

Your thinking can mature over the years.

Each of us is a separate version

You are a "separate version" in your faith and individual relationship with God.

You are your own unique reflection of God's character.

You have your own inner belief system that emphasizes your own personal values and the living out of those values.

You have your own doubts and the living out of those as well.

When you combine your image of God, with your belief system and doubts, you are a unique worshiping human being who is unlike anyone who has ever lived, or ever will.

Respect each other's transitioning and maturing.

Blind spots

Everyone has blind spots. The problem is you can't see them.

Church and culture

Speak your truth in love as you understand it.

Only God knows how things really are.

Start potentially inflammatory comments with qualifiers such as,

> "From my perspective…"

> "You may have a different opinion, but the way I see it is…"

> "Correct me if I am wrong, but…"

This approach restrains bias and dogmatism, and makes room for alternate ideas and their communication.

Me Questions

1. What do you think about the statement, "When you combine your image of God, with your belief system and doubts, you are a unique worshiping human being who is unlike anyone who has ever lived, or ever will"?

    _____

    _____

    _____

2. In what ways has your faith matured over the years? How has this maturing improved your marriage relationship? If it has not improved your marriage relationship, why?

    _____

    _____

    _____

3. What blind spots have you had in the past with regard to marriage?

    _____

    _____

    _____

4. Are there issues in your marriage that you currently refuse to look at? If so, why?

    _____

    _____

We Questions

5. What are your thoughts as a couple on the statement, "Speak your truth in love as you understand it. Only God knows how things really are"?

    _____

    _____

    _____

6. Will both of you commit to using the following qualifiers when expressing your opinions to each other in order to restrain bias and dogmatism, and make room for alternate ideas and their communication? What arguments in the past would have benefitted from these qualifiers?

"From my perspective…"

"You may have a different opinion, but the way I see it is…"

"I could be wrong, but the way I see it…"

"Correct me if I am wrong, but…"

_____

_____

Your Thoughts

_____

_____

_____

_____

_____

_____

_____

_____

_____

_____

_____

Subject: Marriage Sermon on Ephesians 5:21-33 by Josh Miller
Main Points

Singleness is not the waiting room for the main event, which for some is marriage and children.

Singleness is the opportunity to live a powerfully Christ-like life of other-centered love.

Ephesians is written TO and FOR Christians who are filled with the Holy Spirit.

Wives are not told to subordinate themselves to their husband as the unquestioned king of his castle.

The word translated "head"' is kephale, which can have multiple meanings.

One, "Head" means leader/ruler/governor; to be the head means to lead, rule, or govern.

Another, "Head" in ancient Greek means source. When ancient Greek writers would talk about headwaters of rivers, they would use this word as the source.

Still another, "Head" means the most prominent part; not leader/ruler/governor. Paul has already used this word in two of those three ways in Ephesians alone.

Women were disdained and seen as inferior to men in every way in their society.

With regard to household codes, all philosophers were in agreement that husbands were to rule their wives and everything else.

During this same time period, Caesar Augustus, who instituted the Pax Romana, put fines in place for people who stayed single too long, and he had hefty fines for divorce because the empire was falling apart at the seams.

Paul calls for mutual submission with wives, and gentleness with children, and instructs husbands on how to love their wives, not rule over them. This was absolutely counter-cultural at the time.

I will speak to three areas: Sacrificial Love, Sanctifying Love, and Satisfying Love.

Marriage in this section of Ephesians is framed by mutual submission.

Marriage, for too many, is about getting MY needs met.

Marriage is not an 'arms-folded' posture of, "This better be good…" Or, "When YOU start, I'll start."

Marriage is a mutual submission and abandoning to each other. In the 1st century, men would have heard this language and left church with their heads spinning!

Paul pulls back power and control from men, and replaces it with servanthood and love.

Let's look at Spirit-filled submission for husbands.

What does *men* submitting to women look like in marriage?

#1 Sacrificial Love - a husband sacrifices his ego and selfishness to love his wife.

> Husbands, love your wives, just as Christ loved the church and gave himself up for her... (Ephesians 5:25)

For husbands, the call is to sacrificially love their wives in ways that model or reflect the way Jesus loved the church.

Jesus had a *pursuing* love...repeatedly going after outsiders to make them insiders. He pursued those who were caught in sin in order to extend grace to them. His love was proactive.

Jesus loved with a *serving* love.

Jesus had a *burden-bearing* love. He died to take on the sins of other people.

The question for a husband should not be, "How do I get my needs met by this woman?" The question should be the opposite in, "How do I meet the needs of this woman?"

We are to learn from Jesus how to reorient our hearts and submit our egos, desires, and ambition to sacrificially love our wives and make sure that they prosper and flourish.

#2 Sanctifying Love – a husband helps his wife reach her redemptive potential.

When a woman chooses to marry a godly man, the result means she should reach more of her redemptive potential in large part BECAUSE she is married to this man - not in spite of being married to him.

Men, your goal should be to present your wife in all of her splendor to anyone around!

One way to express sanctifying love to your wife is by constantly praying for her.

Pray blessing into her life that God would lighten her load, that she would be filled with joy, full of faith and grace, that God would protect her, and that the kingdom would come more fully in her life.

Sanctifying love draws our wife toward reaching her full redemptive potential.

#3 Satisfying Love – a husband nourishes and cherishes his wife.

> In this same way, husbands ought to love their wives as their own bodies. He who loves his wife loves himself. [29] After all, no one ever hated their own body, but they feed and care for their body, just as Christ does the church— [30] for we are members of his body. [31] "For this reason a man will leave his father and mother and be united to his wife, and the two will become one flesh." (Ephesians 5:28-31)

A husband should nourish and cherish his wife; not be an emotional brute.

Husbands, where there have been words of accusation, we are to speak words of LIFE.

Where there have been words of despair, we are to speak words of HOPE.

A good barometer would be to honestly ask your wife, "On a scale of 1 to 10, how cherished or nourished do you feel from me?" And then listen to her answer.

Then ask, "What can I do to make you feel more cherished and nourished?"

Spirit-filled mutual submission for husbands means we submit our egos, desires, and ambition to the prospering and flourishing of our wives, and cherish them during the process.

Men DO NOT get this vision of marriage from our culture, or most of our families.

> Wives, submit yourselves to your own husbands as you do to the Lord. 23 For the husband is the head of the wife as Christ is the head of the church, his body, of which he is the Savior. 24 Now as the church submits to Christ, so also wives should submit to their husbands in everything. (Ephesians 5:22-24)

How do wives live in mutual submission? What is being asked here?

#1 Submit to their husband's love. Submit means 'to align yourself under something, line up underneath.'

Wives should submit and align themselves to their husband's love, and that love is not about ruling or commanding.

Paul is saying, wives, you are called to *let your husband love you well*, this is what submission is.

Most women are terrified of fully surrendering their heart to another person. Because of the abuses of patriarchy, of how some Christian men have often been arrogant and misrepresented these verses, women often hold something back. This is a fruit of the Fall.

In Genesis 1 and 2, God created man and woman. They were totally equal and given the same commands. Sin entered the world along with something we call 'the Fall.' Sin and the Fall began the distortions and destructive superiority in relationships.

> Genesis 3:16 says, '"I will make your pains in childbearing very severe; with painful labor you will give birth to children. Your desire will be for your husband, and he will rule over you."

Many scholars interpret the word "desire" to mean that Eve will strive to have mastery over her husband. Why would she want this? To guard her heart and protect herself.

For a woman, it is terrifying to let a man see her for who she is because he has the chance to reject her for who she is…which is why some women often hold back.

The call to mutual submission for a wife is to line up under her husband who is sacrificial in his sanctifying and satisfying love for her.

#2 Respect her husband

The only other specific thing mentioned for women in this passage is, "respect her husband."

> However, each one of you also must love his wife as he loves himself,
> and the wife must respect her husband. (Ephesians 5:33)

This verse is also the third time in this section that Paul tells men to love their wife.

Be a strong, humble, tender, mature, secure, loving man; like Christ.

When a man gets a vision for wanting to rise up and lay his life down for his wife, he's going to be awkward when he does it. From vision to execution, there is sometimes a disparity.

Wives, if you see your husband making an effort toward the right direction, give him some respect and encouragement.

Husbands respond to wives who respect and encourage them, and who do not insult or treat them in a condescending way.

Spirit-filled mutual submission for wives, at least in part, looks like letting their husband love them.

If you expect graduate level performance from your husband and get middle school results, being supportive and encouraging will get better results in the future than being critical and condemning.

Cultivate your respect for your husband because you will be staggered by what you reap.

You ask, "How do I do that?" Just as for your husband, you can't on your own. But you can move in that direction because you have the life and power of the Holy Spirit in you.

> This is a profound mystery—but I am talking about Christ and the
> church. (Ephesians 5:32)

When husbands and wives submit to and love each other well, it is a powerful pointer for others toward Christ and the Church. The way I love my wife is pointing to the way Jesus has loved me and loves the Church.

Or, husbands, how about someone asking your wife, "Why do you treat and talk about him like THAT?" And for her to say, "I am modeling something. There is a thing called the Church and it loves Jesus. How I respond to my husband is pointing to THAT. It's a preview of THAT."

A couple of closing thoughts.

There are *no cookie-cutter marriages*. Mutual submission in this way is a huge canvas to paint on.

As a husband or a wife, you are to pay attention to the instructions to YOU.

It is healthy to regularly ask ourselves, "Is my spouse thriving or flourishing? If so, is it in spite of me or because of me?"

Or is your spouse saying:

> "Well, you know, God says in Romans Chapter 8 that all things work together for the good of those who love God; even this marriage. And, in James chapter 1 it says to consider it pure joy when you face trials and tribulations of many kinds because the testing of your faith in this marriage for 18 years has produced fruit."

For those of you who are single, would you pray for married people once in a while?

A 30 day experiment for a husband and wife.

> 1) What would happen if you first submit yourselves to God, and then submit yourselves to each other in the ways described in this passage of Ephesians?

> 2) What new patterns and dynamics would you like to see occur in your marriage in the next 30 days?

If you are married, you need to do the hard work of figuring out a theology and shared philosophy for your marriage. Life is too hard, and there is too much pressure and temptation to NOT go forward UNIFIED.

When we, Josh and Cory Miller, are not in agreement on a decision:

> We press the pause button, pray, wait, and trust God to bring us to unity. This section of Ephesians is far more about unity than authority. If God has made the two of us one, He is big enough to bring us together. If, for some reason we just can't come together, our next step would be asking each other, "Who does this decision affect most?" That would influence our final decision.

Me Questions

1. What are your thoughts on the statement, "Most women are terrified to fully surrender their heart to a man because of abuse, arrogance, distortion, superiority, hierarchy, or patriarchy"?

   _____

   _____

2. What are your thoughts on the statement, "Most men do not have a clue about how to be a man; a strong, humble, tender, mature, secure, and loving man"?

   _____

   _____

Wife

3. Are you terrified to fully surrender your heart to your husband because of abuse, arrogance, distortion, superiority, hierarchy, or patriarchy"? If so, what needs to change?

   _____

   _____

4. In what ways would you like to be nourished and cherished by your husband?

   _____

   _____

5. What does it mean for you to submit and align yourself with your husband's love?

   _____

   _____

   _____

   _____

Husband

6. Is your leadership characterized by abuse, arrogance, distortion, superiority, hierarchy, or patriarchy"? If so, what needs to change? Who can serve as your role model?

    _____

    _____

    _____

7. In what ways do you nourish and cherish your wife?

    _____

    _____

8. Does your leadership and love warrant your wife's submission and alignment? If not, what needs to change?

    _____

    _____

We Questions

9. How many successful marriages can the two of you recall where wives subordinated themselves to their husband as the unquestioned king of his castle? If you can think of any, describe what their success looked like on a day-to-day basis.

    _____

    _____

10. What does mutual submission between a husband and wife mean to the two of you? What are some examples of how this is lived out?

    _____

    _____

11. What does gentleness with children look like? Give examples of how the two of you have given encouragement to your child(ren) and administered discipline.

_____

_____

12. What do both of you think it means for a man to serve his family and lay his life down for them?

_____

_____

13. Does your marriage tell the same relationship story of Jesus and the Church in that people take note and wonder why you live your life together differently? How can you do better?

_____

_____

Your Thoughts

_____

_____

_____

_____

_____

_____

_____

_____

_____

_____

_____

Subject: Re: Marriage Sermon on Ephesians 5:21-33 by Josh Miller; Pursuing Each Other

Main Points

God wants you to be intentional towards your spouse.

God wants you to pursue your spouse in the same way He pursued you with his Son.

God wants you to respond to your spouse in a similar way as He wants you to respond to Him.

Somewhere between boyhood and manhood husbands are suppose to shift from being the pursued, who are cared for by their mother, to being the pursuers who care for their wives, and for that matter, the Church.

Some spouses do not require a lot of pursuing, but what they need, they need.

When a risk becomes a way of life, it feels less and less like a risk.

Children, their families, believers, and people in general are no different even though their culture and financial circumstances may vary.

The first time you suggest something to your spouse to improve your marriage, it may not be believed or received well. Give it time.

The prospect of one spouse leaving on a trip can trigger abandonment issues in the other that originates from an earlier time in his or her life.

It's okay to want someone to go on a missions trip and not want them to leave.

Me Questions

1. What do you think about the statement, "Somewhere between boyhood and manhood husbands are suppose to shift from being the pursued, who are cared for by their mother, to being the pursuers who care for their wives, and for that matter, the Church"?

    _____

    _____

2. What do you think about the statement, "Children, their families, believers, and people in general are no different even though their culture and financial circumstances vary"?

    _____

    _____

We Questions

3. How can you be more intentional towards each other?

    _____

    _____

4. Is each spouse supposed to be the pursuer and the pursued? If so, how does that work in your marriage?

    _____

    _____

5. What would it look like for you to pursue each other in the same way God pursued you with his Son?

    _____

    _____

6. What do you think about the statement, "God wants you to respond to your spouse in a similar way as He wants you to respond to Him"?

    _____

    _____

Your Thoughts

_____

_____

_____

_____

_____

_____

Subject: Re: Re: Marriage Sermon on Ephesians 5:21-33 by Josh Miller; Pursuing Each Other

Main Points

Pursuing

Spouses should equally pursue each other, but do not necessarily have to pursue each other equally.

You need to become the best pursuer of your spouse that you can within the context of your background, strengths, weaknesses, and stage of growth.

When it comes to pursuing each other, there will always be a mismatch between spouses from time to time.

Do not expect your spouse to do all of the heavy lifting in your relationship. Both you and your spouse need to lift what each of you can, and motivate yourselves in a healthy way to do more.

Growth is about what the Holy Spirit wants to do in you without condemning you for who and what you are not.

One of the ways to pursue your spouse is by not *running away* mentally, emotionally, spiritually, or physically.

Sometimes pursuing is merely staying present with your spouse. For a wife this can sound like: "Look at me. Listen to me. Give me a hug. Ask if I need help. Be tender with our children. Tell me about your day or what God has been speaking to you."

Pursuing can be communicating with your spouse about what you are personally struggling with as long as it isn't always and only about you and your struggles.

Learn to pick up on your relationship feelings quickly and know when it is time to check in with your spouse.

Lashing out is not an effective way of communicating a need.

Visibility

Any visibility in life you think you have can just be a mirage.

Do not ignore your health.

Do not ignore warning signs in all areas of your life.

Side note about blood clots: Don't forget to stretch your legs on long flights, or when sitting a lot.

Deserving to be in the Body of Christ

You deserve to be in the Body of Christ only by God's grace and provision.

The Gospels say that the *first will be last, and the last first*. Regardless of where you are in line, make sure you are in the right line!

Ambivalence

Ambivalence means that a person cares strongly about two opposing positions and cannot decide which to do.

To help someone with their ambivalence on an issue, ask gentle, non-condemning, non-condoning questions.

Bring their ambivalence into the open so they can see it more clearly by asking questions about all sides of the decision. Do not debate or argue.

Ask enough questions so the person you are helping can experience outwardly what he or she is struggling with inwardly.

You can use a SWOT analysis to address ambivalence by asking about the Strengths, Weaknesses, Opportunities, and Threats of each choice.

Ambivalence and divorce

Ambivalence regarding divorce can be addressed with questions such as,

"If you stay together, what challenges will you need to work through?"

This could be viewed as a Strength in that Christians would stay together, an Opportunity to build their relationship, and a Threat of continued unfruitful pain if they didn't succeed.

"If you get divorced, what additional challenges will you face?"

This could be viewed as a Strength in that the current pain stops, and a Threat that additional challenges will occur.

"If you get divorced, what pains go away, and what new pains begin?"

This could be viewed as a Strength in that the current pain stops, and a Threat that new pains could occur.

Anger directed inward can result in feelings of depression, or depression itself.

Anger directed *towards you* is not the same as anger directed *at you*.

Sometimes anger needs to be discharged before thinking can begin.

Be committed to do whatever it takes to build a mutually satisfying marriage.

You cannot know what you would do in a situation until it happens to you.

You can be a couple and support each other's healing and growth, or just *act* like a couple and cover up your wounds and pain.

Anger

The spouse who is first to express anger is not necessarily in the wrong.

It can be difficult to notice when people are being aggressive in their passivity.

It's easy for people to see one spouse's anger, yet miss the ways he or she is provoked by the other.

When one spouse communicates feelings in truth and in love, the other should respond with acceptance, affirmation, and encouragement.

You can affirm someone without agreeing. You are just acknowledging that you understand what they think and why.

Walking towards the fire

Be neutrally engaged when someone is angry.

When a spouse is angry, rather than cower and withdraw, stay present and face his or her anger directly. This works for a couple, and not with someone who is an abuser.

Me Questions

1) How natural are you at pursuing your spouse? How can you improve?

2) What do you think about the statement, "One of the ways to pursue your spouse is by not *running away* mentally, emotionally, spiritually, or physically"? Are you prone to running away? If so, why? How can you do better?

3) If lashing out is not an effective way of communicating a need, what is more effective?

4) Do you agree that any visibility in life you think you have can just be a mirage.? Why or why not?

_____

_____

_____

5) How well do you and your spouse take care of your health? Is there room for improvement? It is difficult to have a mutually satisfying marriage when one of you is dead.

_____

_____

6) What do you think about the statement, "No one deserves to be in the Body of Christ, except by God's grace and provision"?

_____

_____

7) Have you experienced anger that when directed inward became depression? If so, how could you have processed and expressed your anger more effectively? Who could help?

_____

_____

_____

8) How difficult is it to discern when your spouse's anger is directed *towards you* rather than *at you*? What does it feel like when either is happening?

_____

_____

_____

_____

We Questions

9) What areas of ambivalence do the two of you have? Remember, this is feeling strongly for two opposite choices.

_____

_____

10) Think about a decision the two of you must make and do a SWOT analysis by asking each other about the Strengths, Weaknesses, Opportunities, and Threats of each option.

_____

_____

11) Are both of you committed to do whatever it takes to build a mutually satisfying marriage? If so, what more needs to change? If not, why?

_____

_____

_____

12) Are you a couple that supports each other's healing and growth, or do you just *act* like a couple and cover up your wounds and pain? If you are acting, what are your thoughts on substituting the *pain of your act* for the *pain of your healing and growth*?

_____

_____

_____

13) According to your rules of engagement, is the spouse who expresses anger first the loser? If so, what are your thoughts on using each other's anger as a possible indicator of a childhood wound that needs to be pursued and healed?

_____

_____

_____

14) How often do either of you use passive aggression as a weapon against the other? If so, does it work? What other options do you have?

_____

_____

_____

_____

15) When one of you communicates feelings in truth and in love, does the other respond with acceptance, affirmation, and encouragement? If not, why?

_____

_____

16) What are your thoughts about the statement, "When a spouse is angry, rather than cower and withdraw, stay neutrally engaged and face his or her anger directly"? Does this work for the two of you? If not, why? Remember, do not do this with an abuser.

_____

_____

Your Thoughts

_____

_____

_____

_____

_____

_____

_____

_____

_____

_____

Subject: Anger and Fire

Main Points

Anger that is unexpressed by one spouse can still be intimidating to the other.

Couples vary in how they handle their anger and arguing. What matters is getting back to connection and peace.

Me Question

1. Does your spouse's anger, expressed or not, intimidate you? If so, why? Is it a repeat of childhood relationships and wounds?

_____

_____

We Question

2. How could the two of you handle anger in your relationship more effectively?

_____

_____

Your Thoughts

_____

_____

_____

_____

_____

_____

_____

_____

_____

_____

Subject: Fight, Flight, Freeze, Submit, or Stand
Main Points

Everyone is "weird" in their uniqueness. An alternate version of Psalm 139:14 could be, "I praise you God because I am fearfully and *weirdfully* made; your works are wonderful, I know that full well."

Patterned reactions

People are who they are for reasons. Unfortunately, some people look at reasons as excuses. They are not excuses; they are insight.

Anyone who was influential during your childhood can contribute to your Imago.

Often what is called a problem is a pattern. Problems can be solved; patterns must be changed. For example, "My pattern of intimidation in the presence of anger isn't only with my spouse."

Fight, flight, freeze, submit, or stand

Social science has known for years that people have a limited number of patterns for responding to a threat.

Five of the responses are fight, flight, freeze, submit, and stand.

Ephesians Chapter 6: 10-20 describes how a Christian should stand firm.

> Finally, be strong in the Lord and in his mighty power. [11] Put on the full armor of God, so that you can take your stand against the devil's schemes. [12] For our struggle is not against flesh and blood, but against the rulers, against the authorities, against the powers of this dark world and against the spiritual forces of evil in the heavenly realms. [13] Therefore put on the full armor of God, so that when the day of evil comes, you may be able to stand your ground, and after you have done everything, to stand. [14] Stand firm then, with the belt of truth buckled around your waist, with the breastplate of righteousness in place, [15] and with your feet fitted with the readiness that comes from the gospel of peace. [16] In addition to all this, take up the shield of faith, with which you can extinguish all the flaming arrows of the evil one. [17] Take the helmet of salvation and the sword of the Spirit, which is the word of God.
>
> [18] And pray in the Spirit on all occasions with all kinds of prayers and requests. With this in mind, be alert and always keep on praying for all the Lord's people. [19] Pray also for me, that whenever I speak, words may be given me so that I will fearlessly make known the mystery of the gospel, [20] for which I am an ambassador in chains. Pray that I may declare it fearlessly, as I should.

When you stand in the power of the Holy Spirit, you do not have to fight, flee, freeze, or submit. You can stand.

Choosing to stand or submit can seem confusing based on what Jesus said in Luke Chapter 6 about what to do with your enemies, and, according to John Chapter 2, what He did to the money changers in the temple.

Luke

"But to you who are listening I say: Love your enemies, do good to those who hate you, 28 bless those who curse you, pray for those who mistreat you. 29 If someone slaps you on one cheek, turn to them the other also. If someone takes your coat, do not withhold your shirt from them. 30 Give to everyone who asks you, and if anyone takes what belongs to you, do not demand it back. 31 Do to others as you would have them do to you. (Luke 6:27-31)

John

When it was almost time for the Jewish Passover, Jesus went up to Jerusalem. 14 In the temple courts he found people selling cattle, sheep and doves, and others sitting at tables exchanging money. 15 So he made a whip out of cords, and drove all from the temple courts, both sheep and cattle; he scattered the coins of the money changers and overturned their tables. 16 To those who sold doves he said, "Get these out of here! Stop turning my Father's house into a market!" 17 His disciples remembered that it is written: "Zeal for your house will consume me." (John 2:13-17)

In Luke, *standing* was manifested by intentionally blessing, praying, and giving even more than what was asked. In John, *standing* was manifested by attacking and driving them out. Both were done only in submission to the will of God in the power of the Holy Spirit.

Prayerfully *stand and give even more*, or *stand and defend*. Either way, speak the truth in love.

Practical tips for responding to someone's anger

Look at the bridge of someone's nose to avoid activating your mirror neurons.

Picture a full-length clear Plexiglas shield between the two of you, with their angry words hitting it like projectile vomit. Put a gutter at the bottom if needed.

Set your phone to speaker and place it two or three feet away. It keeps the person from injecting their venom directly into the center of your head.

Psychologically put on the full armor of God and stand in the power of the Holy Spirit.

Me Questions

1. What do you think about the statement, "Everyone is 'weird' in their uniqueness"?

    _____

    _____

2. Give examples of fight, flight, freeze, submit and stand in your life. What were your reasons for each response. It is important to note that reasons are not excuses; they are insight.

    _____

    _____

We Questions

3. What do the two of you think about the following as it pertains to working through a disagreement? Prayerfully *stand and give even more*, or *stand and defend*. Either way, speak the truth in love.

    _____

    _____

4. Discuss each of the practical tips for responding to someone's anger. Is it okay for the two of you to use them with each other?

    _____

    _____

Your Thoughts

_____

_____

_____

_____

_____

_____

_____

_____

_____

_____

_____

_____

_____

_____

_____

_____

_____

_____

_____

Subject: I Married My Sister!
Main Points

Some people avoid conflict by learning how to anticipate what others want.

Adults need to do what they often tell their children. "Use your words. What are you feeling?"

When you are frustrated or angry ask yourself:

How old do I feel emotionally?

When have I felt this way before?

What is the youngest age I remember feeling this way?

Not sure people ever grow up.

To get your spouse to open up and connect, go on a walk or a drive and be quiet. After a while, ask a question and continue to be quiet. Your time to talk will come.

Men usually do not like being still and face to face when talking. They prefer the less threatening side-by-side walk, or a drive in a car, where they are allowed to keep moving and can look around while listening.

Me Questions

1. Do you spend an inordinate amount of time and energy trying to anticipate what your spouse wants in order to avoid conflict? How successful are you? According to God's economy, is this an effective use of your time and energy?

   _____

   _____

2. How difficult is it for you to use words to express your emotions? If it is difficult, how can you get better at it? How can your spouse help you?

   _____

   _____

   _____

   _____

   _____

   _____

We Questions

3. What do the two of you think about the following strategy? To get your spouse to open up and connect, go on a walk or a drive together, ask a question, and be quiet.

    _____

    _____

4. Is the following true for your relationship?

    Men usually do not like being still and face to face when talking. They prefer the less threatening side-by-side walk, or a drive in a car, where they are allowed to keep moving and can look around while listening.

    _____

    _____

5. What are the best settings and ways for the two of you to communicate?

    _____

    _____

Your Thoughts

_____

_____

_____

_____

_____

_____

_____

_____

_____

Subject: Spinning Plates
Main Points

It is easy to look at others like they are spinning plates on sticks that must be kept spinning or they will fall.

You can be one of your own spinning plates that you ignore until the last minute.

It is not healthy to *need* to be needed.

You might reason that if you are needed, then you are valuable to someone and they won't abandon you.

People often are glad someone is there, not necessarily glad that it is specifically you.

It is fine to *want* to be needed in order to serve God and others in a way that matters, and makes a difference in their lives.

Serving others is being about what God is doing.

When you invest your life in your spouse, you are investing in yourself, your children, and anyone your spouse invests in.

Your spouse, children, and God should not be viewed as spinning plates.

Unless you are intentional, your marriage can feel like just another plate to keep spinning.

Me Questions

1. What spinning plates do you have in your life? Is keeping them spinning causing you to be out of balance? What can you do differently?

_____

_____

2. Do you treat your spouse and children like they are spinning plates? If so, how can you change this so you can connect with them mentally and emotionally in the way God intended?

_____

_____

_____

_____

3. Are you your own spinning plate that you ignore until the last minute? Or, are you fully absorbed with yourself and your spinning? If so, what can you do differently?

    _____

    _____

4. Do you need to be needed in order to value yourself? If so, when did this start? How can you gain a better perspective on serving others?

    _____

    _____

5. In what ways do you serve God and others that makes a difference in their lives?

    _____

    _____

We Questions

6. What do the two of you think about the statement, "When you invest your life in your spouse, you are investing in yourself, your children, and anyone he or she invests in"?

    _____

    _____

7. Do either of you feel like you are a spinning plate in competition with your children and others for your spouse's attention? If so, how can the two of you create a better balance?

    _____

    _____

    _____

    _____

    _____

8. If working on your marriage feels like just another plate to keep spinning, you are not connecting mentally and emotionally with your spouse in the way God intended. Be intentional about finding time to get to know each other. How can the two of you do this?

_____

_____

Your Thoughts

_____

_____

_____

_____

_____

_____

_____

_____

_____

_____

_____

_____

_____

_____

_____

_____

_____

_____

_____

Subject: Unfinished Business
Main Points

People have reasons for being angry at family members and others. It can be even more difficult when those reasons are unknown to others who could help bring about a resolution.

Address issues in your life when you are ready and to the depth you are ready to go.

Me Questions

1. Do you have family members with whom you are angry? If resolution is possible and something you want, seek God about when and how your issues with them can be resolved. That said, begin by continually offering yourself as a living sacrifice to God for the renewing of your mind. Do not do anything until you are ready. Ask a family member or friend for help if they will truly be helpful. What might your first steps be?

   _____

   _____

   _____

2. If your spouse is angry with family members, are you comfortable asking him or her if there is anything you can do to help? If so, do not fall into the trap of trying to fix it. Ask meaningful questions and listen.

   _____

   _____

   _____

We Questions

3. What are the warning signs that conflict is arising from your extended families?

   _____

   _____

   _____

4. How can the two of you help each other deal with conflict in your extended families?

_____

_____

Your Thoughts

_____
_____
_____
_____
_____
_____
_____
_____
_____
_____
_____
_____
_____
_____
_____
_____
_____
_____
_____
_____
_____
_____

Subject: Re: Unfinished Business
Main Points

Talk with family about issues if they are receptive and it can be helpful.

It is important to find someone with whom you can meet regularly to work through difficult issues at your own pace.

Forgiveness is an exchange

Too often well-meaning friends recommend that people cover hurtful family experiences with a "blanket of forgiveness." That may work for a few, but it rarely deals with ongoing consequences, and can be the same as denial and sweeping it under the rug.

To effectively forgive someone, it is best for you to identify exactly what you are forgiving. If you don't, unprocessed details may continue to come to the surface.

Danny Meyer, a Vineyard pastor, teaches in his Gospel of Wholeness series that forgiveness is an exchange with God. You place the offender, offense, and consequences in the hands of God, and He offers His peace and power back to you in return. It is a trade that leaves the offender in God's hands.

A trade with God does not mean you are *letting go* for the offender to run free and not be held accountable. You are giving the offender, the offense, and the consequences to God so you do not have to carry them, or let them be a distraction to you from moving forward with your life. This means that the offender's fate is in God's hands; not your thoughts.

Even if you trade something for God's peace, there are often habitual thought patterns of bitterness that remain. Working to identify these patterns and bring about change takes time, and often requires help from others.

You know you have taken something back from God when you realize that your peace is gone.

Carrying someone else's shame

People often carry the shame of others who are unwilling to accept and carry their own.

Parents do not look at dirt on their child and say, "You are dirt!" Or, "Look at that dirt that oozed out of you!" No. The dirt is *on them, not of them*. This is what wearing inappropriate shame looks and feels like.

Whenever you feel someone else's shame, take it straight to God for a trade. If it is inappropriate shame that was spewed onto you, do not accept it as your own.

Most children who are living in the midst of mentally, emotionally, spiritually, and/or physically dangerous people find it less terrifying to think, "I am bad, and everyone around me is good and loving," rather than, "I am good and everyone around me is bad and dangerous."

It is difficult for children to learn how to handle shame appropriately when others are condemning them and blaming them for things that are not their fault.

Children often carry the shame of the family system and grow into adults who think they are fundamentally bad.

It takes time as an adult to sort through painful memories, own what is yours, reject what is not, ask for forgiveness when appropriate, and place the rest in God's hands.

Family systems really do not like it when their shame bearers refuse to do their assigned job.

Ultimately, you need to take a stand for who God created you to be, and against what others have put on you. As mentioned several times before,

> Therefore, I urge you, brothers and sisters, in view of God's mercy, to offer your bodies as a living sacrifice, holy and pleasing to God — this is your true and proper worship. ² Do not conform to the pattern of this world, but be transformed by the renewing of your mind. Then you will be able to test and approve what God's will is — his good, pleasing and perfect will. (Romans 12:1-2)

The "Do not conform to the pattern of this world" could just as well have been, "Do not *continue to be deformed* to the pattern of this world."

Me Questions

1. Do you need someone to meet with regularly to work through difficult issues regarding your family or spouse? If one counselor does not work out, do not be afraid to keep looking until you find someone who does. What issues would you discuss?

   _____

   _____

2. Have you had well-meaning friends recommend something like a "blanket of forgiveness," without you first working through the specifics of how you were offended and the consequences? If so, how did it feel?

   _____

   _____

3. What are your thoughts on placing an offender, the offense, and the consequences in the hands of God. Does it make sense that He can offer His peace and power back to you in return? It is an exchange.

_____

_____

_____

4. What are your thoughts on your goodness and badness?

_____

_____

_____

5. Do you know anyone who carries the shame of their family system and thinks he or she is fundamentally bad? What would you tell that person?

_____

_____

_____

6. Are you a shame bearer for your family of origin? If so, what would it feel like to refuse?

_____

_____

_____

7. What are your thoughts on the statement, "It takes time as an adult to sort through painful memories, own what is yours, reject what is not, ask for forgiveness when appropriate, and place the rest in God's hands"?

_____

_____

_____

8. What are your thoughts on the statement, "Ultimately, you must take a stand for who God created you to be, and against what others have put on you"?

    _____

    _____

We Question

9. Can the two of you forgive each other by making a trade with God where He takes the offender, the offence, and the consequences in exchange for His peace? If not, why? Learning to forgive is essential for building a mutually satisfying marriage.

    _____

    _____

Your Thoughts

_____

_____

_____

_____

_____

_____

_____

_____

_____

_____

_____

_____

_____

_____

Subject: Re: An Odd Question
Main Points Summary of the Workbook

Happily married couples have disagreements and arguments.

Disagreements do not have to become arguments.

The biggest cause of disagreements is often the chaos of life itself. There is so much going on that you are always pulled in many different directions.

When you and your spouse are tired, frazzled, frustrated, and a disagreement pops up, ask yourselves, "Is it us, or is it life that is draining us?"

Make sure your observing ego has not been a harsh and critical judge with negative and accusing self-talk about the present or past. If so, try to bring grace and truth into your thinking.

When your spouse speaks or answers sharply, you have the choice to either react or respond.

When you are in a disagreement with your spouse, ask yourself, "How do I want this disagreement to end? How do I want our day or evening to go?"

Avoid sliding back into the power struggle.

If you feel out of control and disrespected at work, resist the temptation to come home and be excessively controlling in order to soothe your ego and insecurities.

When you are *demanding* of respect at home, it often means you are not receiving what you think you deserve elsewhere, or even from yourself.

Conflicts should be kept in their own arena. Work conflicts should be dealt with at work, and home conflicts should be dealt with at home.

When you and your spouse find yourselves in an argument, one of you must have the courage to call, "Timeout!" If the other does not heed your agreed upon strategy to avoid hurting each other unnecessarily, then he or she is immediately declared the loser. In essence, the loser is saying, "No! I won't stop arguing! I'm going to keep yelling at you!" That's just childish.

The pride that used to want to win an argument needs to be tied to you obeying your rules of engagement.

Sometimes when you are having an argument, you will need to stop and go through the formal process of letting one person talk with the other mirroring back what was said, which is then followed by asking, "Did I repeat that back correctly?" and "Is there more to that?"

Learn to mentally and emotionally observe yourself and your spouse.

Become comfortable with applying a well-placed hug at the right time.

Learn to not be afraid of each other's anxieties and anger in order to be more fully available to each other.

Healthy couples learn that even if their spouse gets mad, he or she will come back emotionally once things are worked out.

After an argument that is not resolved, the real question is, "How long do you want to stay apart?" It is your choice.

For a couple, personal differences are a combination of their unique expressions of God's character, along with their different areas of healing and growth.

It does no good to try to manipulate your spouse into the image you want.

You need each other's unique expression of God to be fully expressed and experienced together.

Operate from an assumption of trust.

Trust that your spouse has your best interests at heart, and trust that God can heal you when he or she wounds you. This works with couples, not abusers.

Know and understand the core wounds that you and your spouse have.

You cannot make up for your spouse's past wounds, but you can do your best not to reinjure them, or create new ones.

Love your spouse as he or she is, knowing that he or she is striving to become better.

Sometimes you need distance in the form of space and solitude so you can move closer.

Provide time for your spouse to invest with the Lord.

Your spouse is not the enemy.

Vow that it will never be your intent to hurt your spouse.

Be intentional and careful in your interactions.

Be good stewards of each other.

Help each other heal, grow, succeed, and become who God wants you to be.

Be encouragers to each other, not stumbling blocks.

Be partners in each other's healing, growth, and ministry.

Do not be afraid to give each other space to figure out tensions and grumpiness.

Do not pursue your spouse out of your insecurities.

Be patient. When your spouse is ready to talk about something, he or she will.

Ask meaningful questions and wait for answers.

The purpose of questions is to help your spouse think through the answers.

Do not fall into the trap of advice giving.

It is fine to let your spouse know when you are ready to receive input.

Do not pressure yourself to be perfect because perfection is impossible.

When you hear yourself thinking condemning thoughts, reply with a simple, "No thank you."

Your desires and needs are important not only for you, but for your spouse and your relationship as well.

Your desires and needs can be God's whispers into your relationship that are calling your spouse into a place of growth and wholeness where he or she would not have thought to go.

Try to walk with your spouse in the same way Adam and Eve did before the Fall.

You will still suffer from the consequences of the Fall, but you do not have to walk according to them.

Strive for God's will in your marriage as it is in heaven.

There is plenty of praise for both of you from both of you.

Do not wrap your identity in or around your spouse's.

You do not have to be ruled by recurring ineffective patterns from your past.

Stand together. You do not have to fight, flee, freeze, or fearfully submit.

When one of you is weak, the other can be strong for both of you.

> Two are better than one,
>   because they have a good return for their labor:
> [10] If either of them falls down,
>   one can help the other up.
> But pity anyone who falls
>   and has no one to help them up.
> [11] Also, if two lie down together, they will keep warm.
>   But how can one keep warm alone?
> [12] Though one may be overpowered,
>   two can defend themselves.
> A cord of three strands is not quickly broken. (Ecclesiastes 4:9-12)

Look at each day as another day to do marriage better.

Your marriage is a unique expression of the two of you and God in a way that has never been, nor will ever be again.

Be committed to approaching your marriage in the same way that the Apostle

Paul did with his desire to know Christ.

> Not that I have already obtained all this, or have already arrived at my goal, but I press on to take hold of that for which Christ Jesus took hold of me. [13] Brothers and sisters, I do not consider myself yet to have taken hold of it. But one thing I do: Forgetting what is behind and straining toward what is ahead, [14] I press on toward the goal to win the prize for which God has called me heavenward in Christ Jesus. (Philippians 3: 12-14)

Your marriage is part of your heavenward call.

Where you succeed, praise God. Where you fail, trust that your grace and mercy for each other, and His grace and mercy for the two of you is sufficient.

When someday all is said and done, and one of you has to say goodbye to the other, you will want to know that both of you gave everything to your marriage relationship that your flawed selves could give.

Subject: Conflict Checklist
Main Points

The following is a list of questions for you to consider when you are arguing…or more probably afterwards when you try to figure out what happened. It's not a matter of which one of these questions on the list will apply, rather, it's how many.

Conflict checklist

Is it us, or is it the daily pressures of life draining us?

Has our observing ego been condemning us?

Did one of us react rather than respond?

How do we want this disagreement to end?

How do we want our day or evening to go?

Have we fallen back into the power struggle?

Should we call a timeout?

Is our pride trying to "win" or "follow our agreed upon rules of engagement?"

Do we need to take turns talking and mirroring?

Are our fears or anxieties driving our behavior?

Are mental, medical, physical, or hormonal issues contributing to the conflict?

Does one or both of us need physical connection?

Is one of us really mad at or about something else?

Does this conflict involve our unique expressions of the image of Jesus?

Is this a recurring issue or pattern that needs healing and growth?

Have we lost trust in each other?

Is one or more of our core wounds involved?

Have we had enough personal time?

Do we see each other as the enemy?

Am I being a good steward of my spouse?

Does one or both of us need time and space to think?

Is one of us trying to be a fixer for the other?

Are we asking meaningful questions and waiting for answers?

Is either of us caught up in trying to be perfect?

Is this about a valid unmet need or desire?

Is one of us trying to rule over or control the other?

Is one of our strengths perceived as threatening by the other?

Are we taking a stand for what is right and godly?

Has one of us fallen and needs help?

Are we committed to making our marriage better as part of our heavenward call?

Your marriage is under continuous and shifting pressures to which you and your spouse will either react or respond. Just when you think things are sailing along smoothly, bam, something will pop up. And if you are planning or worrying about the future, things can get even more tense when you forget to take Jesus with you into those plans and worries.

Be intentional in your interactions with each other. Your faith in God, His wisdom, and the power of the Holy Spirit is what will deliver and sustain your marriage. Consider putting into practice our adaptation of James 2:14-17.

Original

> What good is it, my brothers and sisters, if someone claims to have faith but has no deeds? Can such faith save them? Suppose a brother or a sister is without clothes and daily food. If one of you says to them, "Go in peace; keep warm and well fed," but does nothing about their physical needs, what good is it? In the same way, faith by itself, if it is not accompanied by action, is dead. (James 2:14-17)

Our adaptation

> What good is it, my brothers and sisters, if Rick and Georgeann claim they want a great marriage but do not work at it? Can lack of effort produce one? Suppose Rick or Georgeann has unmet desires or mental, emotional, spiritual, or physical needs. If one says to the other, "Be happy; keep content, and act fulfilled," but does nothing about those unmet desires or mental, emotional, spiritual, or physical needs, what good is it? In the same way, wanting a mutually satisfying marriage by itself, if it is not accompanied by action, is dead.

God does not give out mutually satisfying marriages, though He is always willing to help His children build them.

ACKNOWLEDGEMENTS

We would like to thank Steve and Katie Helgeson who, during a presentation on marriage at Harvest Vineyard Church in Ames, Iowa, first exposed us to the idea that God's will on earth for marriage was best expressed when He created Adam and Eve, and not after He was forced by their actions to banish them from the Garden of Eden.

Thank you Ann Smiley-Oyen for working through a very early draft, and offering suggestions that considerably and justifiably increased our workload. Your sense of readability and structure is invaluable.

To our early draft and proof readers - We want to thank our youngest daughter Bonnie Mills and Lauren Horsch for their attention to story detail and grammar. We also want to thank Holly Greufe, Amy Gifford, and Kevan Flaming for their many suggestions.

A thank you is also in order for Jerod and Sarita Smeenk and their marriage home group where an early version of this workbook was used for the first time in a group setting. Thank you Becca, our oldest daughter, for your guidance on structure and layout. We would also like to thank Mary L. Martin (Rick's mother) for her meticulous review of the final draft.

We are especially grateful to Stephen Judah of Columbus, Ohio who died June 21, 2008 of esophageal cancer at the age of 59. His marriage weekend seminar that we attended over thirty years ago provided the foundation that the Holy Spirit has used to transform our marriage. We learned of the seminar from our dear friends, Terry and Sue Castor, who cared for us and our three year-old daughter, Becca, during that very intense weekend. Their unwavering support for us personally and for our ministry is deeply appreciated.

We are also grateful to Josh Miller, Senior Pastor at Harvest Vineyard Church in Ames, Iowa, for his vision and support of our ministry. He has the knowledge and wisdom of a skilled teacher and the heart of a loving shepherd.

And finally, to the many couples over the years who have shared the sacred ground of their marriage with us, we are incredibly thankful for your courage, trust, and authenticity before God. Our marriage and life together is far better because of what we have learned from you.

May we all stay faithful on our journey to a mutually satisfying marriage.

In Him,

Rick and Georgeann